THE REFRACTIVE THINKER

AN ANTHOLOGY OF HIGHER LEARNING

Volume Five: Strategy in Innovation

**Edited by
Dr. Cheryl A. Lentz**

The Refractive Thinker® Press

The Refractive Thinker®: An Anthology of Higher Learning
Volume V: Strategy in Innovation

The Refractive Thinker® Press
9065 Big Plantation Avenue
Las Vegas, NV 89143-5440   USA

info@refractivethinker.com
www.refractivethinker.com

Books are available through The Refractive Thinker® Press at special discounts for bulk purchases for the purpose of sales promotion, seminar attendance, or educational purposes. Special volumes can be created for specific purposes and to organizational specifications. Please contact us for further details.

Refractive Thinker® logo by Joey Root, The Refractive Thinker® Press logo and cover design by Jacqueline Teng, final production by Gary A. Rosenberg.

Printed in the United States of America

10   9   8   7   6   5   4   3   2   1

Contents

The important thing is not to stop questioning.
Curiosity has its own reason for existing.
One cannot help but be in awe when he contemplates
the mysteries of eternity, of life,
of the marvelous structure of reality.
It is enough if one tries merely to
comprehend a little of this mystery every day.
Never lose a holy curiosity.

—ALBERT EINSTEIN (1879–1955)

Foreword

Rapidly evolving technology has created a chaotic business environment, challenging every business on its journey to success. Chaos is not simply a theory, but a ubiquitous, necessary and rapidly changing element in navigating today's business world. During periods of market turbulence, this disorder has proven to be the arbiter of success. Those who can deal with change flourish. Those that cannot adapt become extinct.

Refractive thinking will help you mollify market turmoil by helping you strike a balance between the need for order and the imperative to change. Refractive thinking is a key to surviving in a chaotic environment, enabling you to establish an innovative comfort zone within its extremes. A business is functioning at its optimum capability when it can generate and apply enough innovation to keep its operating systems vibrant, yet keep it from collapsing into anarchy.

Finding and maintaining this zone in a complex, competitive business system is a delicate matter. If uncontrolled momentum carries people too far from its center, they risk falling into inconsistency and dissolution. And if the system moves too far in an opposite direction the entrepreneur faces rigidity. A business can survive in a constantly changing environment by becoming the driving force of controlled change, applying refractive thinking to extend the corporate life cycle, preparing the business to compete successfully during the current technological explosion.

Change is not prompted by companies, but by the people in them. And because every business is made up of people, the corporate comfort zone is comprised of the collective beliefs of its individual decision makers. Unfortunately, many business people find that thinking for themselves can be an uncomfortable process. Most simply repeat what they have been told and become upset if they are exposed to a different view.

Conversely, significant benefits accrue to the astute refractive thinkers who can change their focus, acclimatize to change and grow their businesses. The bottom line is an improved bottom line, since these benefits translate into greater profitability for your business. Refractive thinking in itself is not a source of change. But *applied* refractive thinking is a compelling element of productive growth. The power of an idea—properly developed and implemented—can liberate you and your business to greatness.

Beliefs guide behavior, which has evolutionary importance among business people. Behavior can be planned, but not directed. Personal performance happens spontaneously, but can also be self-organizing. People, and subsequently their companies, must apply refractive thinking, adapt an innovative behavior or be swept aside.

By definition, innovation implies risk. Refractive thinking is an unknown ally that leads us willingly into unknown territory. Refractive thinking is the sounding buoy that guides us through the future fog. And therein lies the inherent opportunity of refractive thinking. As we move into the future, we can see more clearly about us, gain our bearings and advance, one creative step at a time. Those who proceed without forethought and care may end up on the rocks.

Refractive thinking acts as a GPS, keeping us moving in the right direction on the path to success. Innovation in itself does not eliminate risk or lead us toward achievement. Success occurs with the application of creativity, within the confines of a chaotic environment, enabling us to create opportunities and manage risk. This volume in The Refractive Thinker® series will help you integrate refractive thinking into your core strategies to deliver strategic value under varying conditions. By so doing, you can drive revenue growth and secure long-term secure competitive advantage.

Brian Jud

Brian Jud is the author of
How to Make Real Money Selling Books
and *Beyond the Bookstore.*

Preface

I *think* therefore I am.
—RENEE DESCARTES

I *critically think* to be.
I *refractively think* to change the world.

Welcome to *The Refractive Thinker®: Volume V: Strategy in Innovation.*

Thank you for joining us for the Fall 2010 edition, Volume V, as we continue to celebrate the accomplishments of doctoral scholars affiliated with many phenomenal institutions of higher learning. The purpose of this offering in the anthology series is to share another glimpse into the scholarly works of these participating authors, specifically on the topic strategic thought in innovation.

In addition to exploring various aspects of innovation, the purpose of *The Refractive Thinker®* is to serve the tenets of leadership. Leadership is not simply a concept outside of the self, but comes from within, defining our very essence; where the search to define leadership becomes our personal journey not yet a finite destination. *The Refractive Thinker®* is an intimate expression of who we are—

the ability to think beyond the traditional boundaries of thinking and critical thinking. Instead of mere reflection and evaluation, one challenges the very boundaries of the constructs itself. If thinking is *inside* the box, and critical thinking is *outside* the box, we add the next step of refractive thinking, *beyond* the box. Perhaps the need exists to dissolve the box completely. As in our first four volumes, the authors within these pages are on a mission to change the world, never satisfied or quite content with *what is* or asking *why*, instead these authors intentionally strive to push and test the limits to ask *why not*.

Peter Senge (1994) in his book, *The Fifth Discipline Fieldbook* wrote:

> Herein lies the strongest reason to look for tools based on important new theories: only such tools have the power to change how we think. Most tools introduced into management to solve problems, however innovative they may be, are based on conventional ways of thinking . . . To paraphrase Albert Einstein, our present problems cannot be solved at the level of thinking at which they were created. (Senge, 1994, p. 31)

This argument offers yet another perspective that supports that when "relying on our present ways of thinking, it is very difficult to develop tools that change the way of thinking. For this we must find or generate new theory" (Senge, 1994, p. 31). The goal of Volume V authors is to use refractive thinking to discover new ways of looking at current or old ideas, in new ways, and with new structure for learning and contemplation. The goals of this volume are to offer alternatives these authors choose to take and to share with you their reasons why, to translate this understanding into innovations in theory, in design, in infrastructure, in organizational culture, within competition, within academic programs, and concerning the area of homelessness.

We look forward to your interest in discussing future opportunities. Let this collection of authors continue our journey begun with volume I to which *The Refractive Thinker®* will serve as our guide to future volumes. Come join us in our quest to be refractive thinkers and add your wisdom to the collective. We look forward to your stories.

Please contact The Refractive Thinker® Press for further information regarding these authors and the works contained within these pages. Perhaps you or your organization may be looking for their expertise to incorporate as part of your annual corporate meetings as a key note or guest speaker(s), perhaps to offer individual, or group seminars or coaching, or require their expertise as consultants.

Join us on this next adventure of *The Refractive Thinker®* where Volume V continues the discussion specifically begun in Volume I with leadership, II with Research Methodology, III with Change Management, and IV with Ethics, Leadership, and Globalization, themed to explore the realm of strategic thought, creativity, and innovation.

Acknowledgments

The foundation of leadership embraces the art of asking questions—to validate and affirm *what* we do and *why*. Leaders often challenge this status quo, to offer alternatives and new directions, to dare to try something that has not yet been done as again proved true in this case with Volume V. This publication required the continued leap of faith and belief in this new publishing model by those willing to continue forward on this voyage. As a result, please let me express my gratitude for the help of the many that made this project possible.

First, let me offer a special thank you to Trish Hladek for her unwavering support and belief that traversing unchartered waters is worthy of the journey. My gratitude extends to our Peer Review Board to include: Dr. Tom Woodruff, Dr. Laura Grandgenett, and Dr. Elmer Hall; and our Board of Directors to include: Dr. Elmer Hall, Dr. Edward Knab, Dr. Judy Blando, Dr. Lisa Kangas, Dr. Tom Woodruff, (and myself); as well as our production specialist, Gary Rosenberg; Refractive Thinker® logo designer, Joey Root; and our cover and companion website designer, Jacqueline Teng.

Let me also extend my sincere thanks to all participating authors within The Refractive Thinker® Project who continue to believe in this project as we continue to expand our program. We appreciate their commitment to leadership and to the concept of what it means to be a refractive thinker.

Dr. Cheryl A. Lentz
Managing Editor
Las Vegas, NV
November, 2010

CHAPTER 1

Innovation Out of Turbulence: Scenario and Survival Plans that Utilizes Groups and the Wisdom of Crowds

Dr. Elmer B. Hall

As the smoke in the Gulf of Mexico starts to clear and the economy slowly claws its way out of the Great Recession, companies are going back to the drawing board to plan for survival and to build strategies for innovation out of the destruction. One type of group planning, scenario planning, is considered to be more important during the recent recession according to the 2009 McKinsey study (Dye, Sibony, & Viguerie, 2009). All types of planning, including disaster planning, should be tied into the process of innovation. In addition, the wise use of teams, both groups and crowds, has to be part of that process. This article will address these topics: a) a disaster before if happened; b) strategic planning process; c) survival planning; d) the planning failures of BP, the oil industry and government; e) scenario and cross-functional team planning; f) non-sustainable issues and looming scenarios; g) innovation: using groups and experts; h) innovation: the wisdom of crowds, a missed opportunity; and, i) conclusions. Additionally, Appendix A analyzes *group collaboration using Wikipedia.*

This article uses BP PLC (BP) as the perfect case study of normal planning gone wrong. Not only should BP management have done better planning, but they also missed significant opportunities for collaboration and innovation.

Note that this article makes extensive use of Wikipedia, which is probably the world's greatest collaboration success story (Alexander, 2008; Friedman, 2009; Gloor, 2005; Howe, 2009; Tapscott & Williams, 2006; Wikipedia Foundation, Inc. [WF], 2010). The sections of Wikipedia used for this article were current, fact-filled, and appeared to be accurately cited in most cases as discussed in Appendix A and illustrated in Table 1. Note the richness, depth and recentness of all the pages—called *articles*—in the table. Appropriately, this article about group innovation cites Wikipedia; and, in each case, the cited topics are article listings in Table 1 and cited in the text as *WF, 2010, topic,* including Wikipedia itself (WF, 2010, Wikipedia).

A Disaster Before It Happened

Scenario planning—and disaster recovery plan (DRP) development—seeks to identify possible outcomes of the future actions that will impact the organization (WF, 2010, scenario plan, DRP). Planners consider the likelihood and the impact of something happening. Managing the risks includes generating options to minimize, avoid, mitigate and develop contingency plans for possible outcomes (WF, 2010, BCP). Year 2000 (Y2K) planning is an excellent example of companies practicing scenario and contingency planning (Hall & Hinkelman, 2007).

Scenario-type planning would have helped with the great BP oil spill in the Gulf of Mexico that blew in April of 2010. Scenario planning should have identified and escalated the level of risk and the likelihood of failure of (deep-water) drilling in the Gulf, resulting in more caution and better preventative measures. Reviewing safety records in the Gulf showed that there were hundreds of oil spills since 2001 (WF, 2010, oil spills), especially those associated with the active hurricane seasons of 2004 and 2005. Part of the scenario planning process would have looked at minimizing the impact of a disaster. This would have and should have resulted in updates to the Disaster Recovery Plans of BP, its business partners, the industry, and the government. All of these DRPs appear to have been disasters in waiting (AP, 2010; BP, 2010; Snyder, 2010; WF, 2010, BCP, DRP, Horizon Deepwater oil spill).

Strategic Planning Process

First, how would strategic planning likely be done under ideal, *normal* conditions? In *Perpetual Innovation: A Guide to Strategic Planning, Patent Commercialization, and Enduring Competitive Advantage,* Hall and Hinkelman (2007) developed an organization-wide planning process that works backward from a key annual event faced by all organizations: end-of-year tax reporting. Most companies finalize a business plan, or at least a budget, in the last quarter of the fiscal

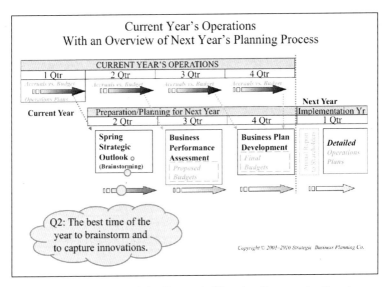

Figure 1: Overview of the Strategic Planning Process by Quarter
(used with author permission)

year as shown in Figure 1 (Hall & Hinkelman, p. 20). Besides all the state and federal taxes that are due at the end of the fiscal year (or immediately thereafter), organizations need to develop *annual report* for their shareholders. Once the business plan and associated budget are finalized for the new year, everyone in the organization must go about the implementation of that plan for the upcoming year. Working backwards from the end-of-year plans, Figure 1 shows how the planning process could be done for a larger organization to culminate in the integrated *corporate business plan.* The third quarter is when all of the forecasting for the year and proposed budget for next year can be developed from each department. Backing up one more quarter to the second quarter, the spring is the best time to do brainstorming and longer-term planning.

For larger companies, there could be many sub plans developed including plans for each division or line-of-business (LOB). Collectively, these various plans are likely integrated into a high-level strategic plan (StratPlan). Every company has its own planning process. Often they are not very formalized, especially for small companies. Many planning activities, like new product development including Intellectual Property (IP) protection with Research and Development (R&D) have to take a much longer view and must be prioritized in annual budgets over several years. That prioritization process needs to balance short-term and long-term goals of the organization. Hall and Hinkelman (2007) recommend *scenario planning* every 2 or 3 years to strengthen the business plan and to provide flexibility if one of the alternate scenarios of the future starts to form.

Scenario Planning

A McKinsey study in 2009 found that 81% of companies had changed their planning process with more than 50% adding or expanding scenario analysis to take on a more prominent role.

In a highly uncertain environment, the advantages of scenario planning are clear: since no one base case can be regarded as probable, it's necessary to develop plans on the assumption that several different futures are possible and to focus attention on the underlying drivers of uncertainty. (Dye, Sibony, & Viguerie, 2009, p. 1)

Long-term planning, or horizon planning, is nothing new to capital-intensive companies such as manufacturers, utilities, and (some) urban planners. Hall and Hinkelman (2007) built a more robust horizon planning process that integrates scenario planning (2007, Chapter 10). This process draws out multiple possible futures, not just the *official future* that most companies use with straight-line trend projections (Schwartz, 1996; WF, 2010, scenario plan). The official view is almost always biased to the view of top executives who are usually the visionary forces in the organization. Therefore, scenario planning is an imperative for creating planned alternatives for major possible futures. Scenario planning looks at the various *drivers* that might lead to a future other than the official one. In so doing, early warning signs can be identified that an alternative scenario of the future is starting to become more likely, and to develop contingency plans for that eventuality. Royal Dutch/Shell Company, one of the earliest and most aggressive users of scenario planning, looked for the rise of a moderate, Mikhail Gorbachev, to power in Russia as the indication that the communist state would fall and that the vast oil/gas reserves of the Union of Soviet Socialist Republics (USSR) would consequently reach the world market (Schwartz, 1996). With Russian and other oil on the market, Shell correctly predicted the several decades of cheap oil in world markets (Schwartz, 1996).

"Scenarios are stories, they are creative writing, but they are not science fiction. The process or incremental steps to creating scenarios use facts and plausible outcomes" (Anderson, 2010, p. 49). As business plans for the year are finalized, these plans should be played against the various scenarios of the future. This means that more flexible alternatives will be chosen over the ones that would be most profitable in the *official future* but not in other scenarios. Another advantage of scenario planning is that DRPs and Business Contingency/Continuity Plans (BCPs) are based on the more visual depictions from the scenario story lines of what each scenario could bring. In the Year 2000 (Y2K) preparation, for example, contingency plans were integrated in many cases with existing DRPs associated with disaster planning that shut down buildings or interrupted suppliers.

Consequently, scenario plans need to be developed prior to a major or catastrophic event. Hall and Hinkelman (2007) addressed several scenario plans:

- *Y2K.* The Y2K event was a massive exercise in computer systems evaluations and upgrades. Y2K planning included the evaluation of business partner risks and focus on those issues that could be most catastrophic (p. 158).

- *Socialized Healthcare.* Based on runaway healthcare costs, Hall and Hinkelman developed *The New Era in Healthcare is Upon Us!* scenario (p. 169). Taking several geopolitical issues into consideration, this scenario anticipated the rise of Hillary Clinton to power based on a socialistic movement.

- *Zero gravity in the housing market.* The *MIL Addition* scenario looked at the supersonic growth in property values from a local government's point of view. The property tax rate for most states is based on the *milage* rate (a *mil* is one thousandth or 0.01% of the assessed value of the property). The doubling of home values over a couple of years meant that the taxes doubled (for those properties without some type of homestead exemption). Several basic projections of rapid property growth demonstrated how unsustainable the property value appreciation was. The author's chose just one possible manifestation of the problem (p. 171).

- *Hurricanes.* In 2004, Hinkelman drafted a scenario related to urban development and disaster planning (although it was never published). The hypothetical city was a peninsular urban setting with ocean access and only one bridge. One year later, a similar scenario unfolded—in fact, an eerie, worst case—when Katrina came ashore in New Orleans!

Scenario planning is a very useful tool for looking at an uncertain future and non-sustainable trends and drawing logical conclusions of the future from them. Scenario themes should be: "relevant, plausible, unique, and challenge the status quo or *official view of the future*" (Hall & Hinkelman, 2007, p. 164). The 2009 McKinsey study found that Chief Executive Officers (CEOs) plan to make much greater use of scenario planning after the Great Recession. Currently, however, many companies are still in survival mode.

Survival Planning

Once a disaster happens, the disaster or contingency plans need to be executed. But many companies do not have such contingency plans; or, if they do, the plans are often painfully inadequate—as evidenced by BP, which was saving walruses and waking up long-dead experts as part of their Gulf DRPs (AP, 2010). Under emergency conditions, a rapid planning approach must be launched that uses prior plans to the extent that they are useful and creates new plans of attack with strategies for survival. Hall (2009b) discussed survival planning in detail. A post mortem analysis allows the strategic planning team to determine what from the prior plans should be retained and what should be abandoned. "Since the *official view* is no longer true, what has changed and what is the new official view, if there is one?" (Hall, 2009b, p. 51). The past situational analysis, typically a strengths-weaknesses-opportunities-threats (SWOT) analysis, might only need to be adjusted to have different rankings that shift priorities under the new reality. Using the current analysis, new strategies need to be formulated for the organization. *The Commercialization of Patent Assets* (COMPASS®) approach developed by Hall and Hinkelman (2007) for high-tech firms continues to work well through all planning scenarios; COMPASS® produces different results under conditions of survival planning. For governments, the Analysis of Innovation and Major Industries to Target (AIMIT™) approach developed by Hall (2007) would help the government and the community to focus on the best industries and companies to promote.

In the end, the survival plan can be developed quickly and provides at least a preliminary plan to move beyond the crisis. A high-level StratPlan and a Survival Plan are two likely components of the plan for survival (Hall, 2009b). The survival plan needs to maintain the organization's core competencies and competitive advantages; it must leave the organization strong enough to compete another day: adapting and innovating simply to stay alive.

The Planning Failures at BP, the Oil Industry and Government

BP, the government, and the oil industry were painfully ill prepared for an oilrig failure, especially in deep-water (AP, 2010; Power, Kell, & Hughes, 2010; WF, 2010, Deepwater Horizon oil spill, oil spills). Companies and governments have practice drills as a critical part of disaster recovery planning. A DRP is only as good as the people who use them. Schools have fire drills, airlines have security drills, and consumer companies have *saving-the-brand* drills where they engage people from all functional areas of the company within minutes of an event that could affect health, safety and, of course, the *brand*. In these trial runs, procedures from the DRP and from contingency plans are reviewed (WF, 2010, DRP, BCP). The plans are updated after each drill.

At least in deep water, BP and Deepwater Horizons apparently had no real contingency plan at all if the blowout preventer failed (Mason, 2010). As Rep. Joe Barton (a Republican from Texas) said during one of the endless government hearings on the spill disaster, "You can't have a contingency plan that says cross your fingers and hope. . . We need more than a cookie cutter contingency plan" (Power, 2010, para. 20).

If scenario planning had been conducted, attention would have been drawn to the 2007 Mineral Management Service study that summarized the horrible history of safety in off-shore drilling including 126 blowouts (average of three blowouts per year for 40 years) on the Outer Continental Shelf since 1971. Mexico's Ixtoc Gulf blowout flowed for 290 days. Scenario planning for the oil industry would almost certainly have recommended regulation, self-regulation, and/or elimination of the Jones Act that prohibits the US from accepting other countries' help during such a disaster. Maybe the limit on the possible fines to an oil company of $75 million skewed the risk decisions of oil companies (EPA, 2010).

Apparently, several other oil companies had contingency plans that were carbon copies of each other, including the same references to walruses and other non-Gulf considerations as well as the some of the same long-dead experts (AP, 2010). The oil industry itself probably should have developed and tested contingency plans that are global in nature with regional modifications. This is actually what has happened; in July 2010, four of the other big oil companies (not BP) contributed $1B to a new non-profit organization to respond to oil fires and spills (Coombs, 2010).

The EPA had updated the National Contingency Plan guidelines in January 2010 related to a massive oil spill, or similar type of catastrophe (EPA, n.d.). The plan describes that there will be a *National Response System* that engages and coordinates all the entities involved. The EPA manual discusses the importance of testing a completed DRP response plan and including an exercise or drill to assess how well it might work when needed (EPA, 2010, chapter 7).

So the industry, BP, and the EPA—including the Mine Safety & Health Administration (MSHA)—had woefully inadequate contingency plans (AP, 2010; BP, 2010). Their plans lacked adequate response team formation as well, meaning that the ability to create a plan on-the-fly was seriously impaired.

Scenario and Cross-Functional Team Planning

Scenario planning would have helped with developing a more robust contingency plan. Engaging cross-functional teams and experts could also have been used immediately after the event to best address and coordinate all of the planning, logistics, and recovery plans. Apparently a cross-functional team should best be developed by one or more industry associations. A disaster response company is now being created by the big oil companies (Coombs, 2010). At least some of the teams could be developed in a Delphi-type of approach using a cross-discipline team with deep expertise in several areas (Hall, 2009a). The team would need to include, at a minimum, government representation, including EPA, mining regulation and enforcement, economic, financial, and technical expertise in engineering, drilling, environmental groups. This type of focused planning should probably be done every couple years.

The outcomes from such team activities and scenario planning include:

1. Identifying possible outcomes within the industry due to natural disasters, geopolitical, accidents, terrorism, etc.

2. Assessing the magnitude and likelihood of possible outcomes

3. Prioritizing the most important and most actionable of these outcomes

4. Estimating which are the most important

5. Communicating the findings to all concerned: government, industry, affected companies, and environmental groups

6. Developing contingency plans for the industry, for government, and recommendations for DRPs for companies

7. Testing the plans and making revisions

Possible findings from the Gulf oil spill could have (should have) been that: regulations and inspections were lax; the likelihood of spills are high (100 to 200 in the gulf per decade); the likelihood of massive spills somewhere in the world is high (every year or so); and, the ability of the world to respond to massive spills is weak (WF, 2010, oil spills). Recommendations from such an analysis might include: global and integrated response teams; recommendations for more safety or contingency measures by increased regulation, increased emphasis from corporations and/or industry-wide self-regulation; marketing and legal response teams.

Yes, scenario planning and disaster recovery planning conducted prior to the oil spill would have been nice. Yes, such planning might have helped avert the disaster in the first place. But additionally it would have also helped with a coordinated response, left a rapid response team in place, and provided a more efficient way of communicating with the public that did the best job of protecting the brand and minimizing legal risks.

Verification at so many levels was missing before, during, and after the spill. BP's estimates of the oil being spilled were embarrassingly low to people watching the satellite images or the live spill cam (WF, 2010, Deepwater Horizon). Additionally, Gulf residents trying to mitigate the damage were especially frustrating. The inability of BP and the government to coordinate various responses is of special interest for people considering the *lessons learned* from this disaster.

Non-Sustainable Issues and Looming Scenarios

As in the case where a large oil spill disaster is inevitable and should be planned for, there are several areas where scenario planning should probably be best done at the highest level of government, industry, and corporations. There are industries where most people are set in believing that the future, the *official future,* is something that is far more strongly tied to the past than to the likely futures. That is, people basically draw a trend line foreword from the past to get the most likely future that results in *bubbles* (WF, 2010, economic bubble). Bubbles are trends that reinforce themselves into non-sustainable trajectories. The Dot-Com and the housing bubbles are two examples that contributed to the last two recessions. Unfortunately, in some cases, the official view may be the least likely of the three or four future scenarios in scenario planning. Here are some examples.

1. At some point soon, maybe 20 years, the silicone chip should hit a brick wall in terms of the ability to be miniaturize, according to Moore's law—half the size and twice the computing power occurs every 18 months (Jordan, 2010). A new technology will need to replace silicone at some point. This should shake up the computing industry and the companies with the patents may become the new rulers of the new computer-processing world.

2. The federal deficit, combined with the perpetual trade deficits, has created an unsustainable condition (WF, 2010, Recession of

2008). The three ways to solve the deficit are: economic growth, increased taxes, and reduced government spending. Rapid economic growth in the US that usually follows a recession is not occurring; growth has been lethargic. That leaves spending cuts and raising taxes which are both politically difficult. David Walker (2010) the former head of the US Government Accounting Office will talk with anyone and everyone who will listen about starting to address the looming fiscal problems of the US. Inflation is virtually guaranteed, the question is how soon.

3. Medicare, Medicaid, and heath care in general are a huge and ever growing percentage of the US GDP. The healthcare bill of 2010 did little to address this unsustainable trend. The US spends about twice as much and gets about half as much healthcare as other developed countries. The US is overspending on healthcare compared to other countries, and this is impeding the country's competitive position (Johnson, 2010).

4. There are several megatrends in the oil and coal industry that should be looked at to develop scenarios of the future:

   • *Peak oil* is widely discussed in the industry that there is a peak level at which oil can be produced (WF, 2010, peak oil). Oil fields are depleted at a rate that requires about 4% more oil to be found each year to stay even. Countries such as the United Kingdom, United Arab Emirates (UAE), Mexico and others are well past their peak production and in rapid decline. Some experts believe that the maximum world production of oil is about 85 million barrels per day (mbpd) (WF, 2010, peak oil). So it is possible that supply constraints will cause the price of oil to skyrocket as the world economy recovers, especially if countries revisit their oil/energy consumptive ways. (Bentley & Boyle, 2008; DiPeso, 2005; Kaufmann, 2008; Roger, 2009).

- *Peak coal* is a similar situation that might occur much sooner this century than anticipated; the maximum production may be occurring now (Cernansky, 2010).

- The *true costs of oil and coal* are likely much higher than what people in the US are paying at the pump/meter. The Gulf spill might lead consumers and governments to reevaluate the externality costs of oil and coal. The Gulf explosion killed 11 people, but thousands of coal miners die each year, especially in China and Russia (WF, 2010, mining accidents). There are hundreds of thousands of people who die from the smog and pollution associated with burning fossil fuels. In the US an estimate is 13,500 die each year and heath care costs are $100B associated with the pollution from coal (Matthews, 2010). Despite all the mine deaths, injuries and air pollution from coal, coal has other dirty secret: coal ash (Kromm, 2010). Given these massive spillover costs to society, various reactions of consumer groups and governments are possible, maybe even probable—especially when considering coal's dominant contribution to global warming.

- If *global warming* gets thrown into the mix with taxes or cap and trade, the future for coal and oil can get fuzzy quickly (EPA, n.d.; IPCC, 2007; UNFCCC, n.d.). Most of the countries that signed onto the Kyoto protocol have made significant progress related to pollution and greenhouse emissions (WF, 2010, global warming, climate change). Even as the science becomes clearer and the impacts of climate change more drastic, several countries —especially China, the US, India, and Russia—are still making very feeble steps of progress.

5. *Hot, Flat, and Crowded* by Thomas Friedman (2009) addresses three super, megatrends: global warming issues combined with flattening of the world technologically as well as population growth. Friedman tries to project what these major forces produce

when all three of them go past the *tipping point.* With the possibility of anyone anywhere being able to develop their ideas and to propagate them globally, there is an unprecedented ability for collaboration in ways that have never been used before. Friedman talks about the removal of governments, countries, and even companies as controlling points in this avalanche of ideas and productivity. People can take their ideas, software and music directly to the end consumer.

Just when people are starting to get used to the idea of *Cloud Computing,* there is *Cloud Computing 2.0* (WF, 2010, cloud computing). These combined forces represent a wonderful topic for a scenario planning session for almost any industry or company. In looking at some of the likely areas that could divert the future of many organizations from the *official future,* governments and industry associations could do more to develop potential scenarios and to develop triggers that would warn people and organizations that the road ahead has changed, and the ride is about to get bumpy.

Innovation: Using Groups and Experts

Besides, in scenario planning, groups and experts can go a long way in innovation. Hall and Hinkelman (2007) describe the use of cross-functional teams, which they call Enabling Technology Unit (ETU) teams at early stages of technology development. Once the technology is ready for commercialization, the ETU teams hand off to the product development teams who bring the new technology to market. The Hall-Hinkelman planning process is very detailed since it is designed for comprehensive planning in larger organizations. Smaller organizations will use less formal planning and will tend to have smaller, more agile, teams. All this use of teams and planning helps to provide efficient channels to bring inventions to commercial success. Many of the tools, especially horizon, scenario, and survival planning, help to focus innovative attention on a major problem or an industry-changing event. Quality teams can help focus people's attention on the most important, actionable, root cause of a problem.

Research on the effective use of teams is summarized well by Straus, Parker, Bruce and Dembosky (2009). Such issues as *group think* and *productivity loss* can often be reduced if care is used in determining when to use individuals versus groups. Also, the way in which teams are formed and operated can help improve their success. A Delphi technique can be used very effectively in many cases to help minimize many of the negative effects of group analysis (Hall, 2009a).

In the case of BP, various types of scenario or Delphi planning probably would have allowed BP to more quickly revive the planning teams that had been used previously. The formation of new teams takes time, time that was at a premium as the disaster unfolded. BP was especially ill prepared to deal with the avalanche of ideas that came in after the disaster.

Innovation: BP's Use of Crowds, a Missed Opportunity!

"Necessity, who is the mother of invention"

—PLATO (c. 380 BC)

The worst oil disaster in history created unprecedented necessities: stopping the leaking deepwater well, cleaning up what was being spilled, and minimizing the environmental damage, to name a few (WF, 2010, Deepwater Horizon oil spill). Not only was BP barraged with lawsuits, investigations, and media inquiries, but also the company was overwhelmed with suggestions. Within 2 months of the Great Oil Spill, BP had more than 60,000 ideas submitted to them (Reyes, 2010). Some 8,000 of these ideas were detailed. YouTube videos popped up with individuals and companies demonstrating the experiments of their innovations. Years may pass before these ideas are fully vetted.

InnoCentive, and organizations that specializes in using its groups of 200,000 "solvers" to address tough problems, presented ideas to BP and proposed to work closely with them to help solve the problems of the disaster (Walker, 2010). InnoCentive proposed 809 solutions, but BP did not follow through with accepting their ideas or their *crowdsourcing* support.

Probably no company faced with a disaster like the one in the Gulf is prepared to handle such a deluge of ideas. Collaborative systems, however, should enable them to do so. An example in the face of disaster is people trying to locate each other after Hurricane Katrina in 2005; volunteer programmers created KatrinaList.com (PeopleFinder) within 4 days and then more than 3,000 participants help coordinate the integration of all the looking-for-people ads in all the different source such as CraigsList and Yahoo to create one mega list of people trying to find loved ones (Reyes, 2010).

A collaborative system that would be generic and could easily be customized for different disaster situations should probably have the following characteristics:

- A *submission process* is the first thing needed to accept ideas. If patenting is necessary before the innovation is exposed to the group/crowd, then a rapid patenting process using provisional patents might be employed (see Hall & Hinkelman, 2007).

- The *first level review* might take the form of Wikipedia where submissions are reviewed before they become published and anything published can be edited and/or recommended for removal.

- A *ranking and prioritization system* would help to get the proposals reviewed by volunteers. The ranking system could work like eBay where there is an overall rating but detailed categories are also allowed. YouTube and other sites indicated popularity based on the number of times viewed.

- Response teams to bring together the best solutions within each of several categories should review a *best ideas list.*

- A *final review team* could be given presentations by the idea originators/inventors. Volunteers and/or employees could also help create the final analysis for each idea.

- The winners would have to have more *detailed plans* developed, and they would have to include probability estimates of success, and cost-benefit analysis.

- Lastly, an *implementation team* would have to go about implementing the winning ideas.

- A *post implementation review* and analysis would provide feedback to the crowd, and close the feedback loop.

Using the wisdom of crowds (Surowiecki, 2005), *open innovation* or *crowdsourcing* (Howe, 2009) should be exceptionally useful for handling the massive inflow of ideas like happened in the Gulf disaster. But these filtered ideas then need to be integrated into the Survival Plan.

In an always connected, interactive world, people anywhere and everywhere can be brought together to help solve general problems, or specific ones. The wisdom of crowds should not be underestimated (Alexander, 2008; Howe, 2009; Sawyer, 2007; Suroweicki, 2008). The ability to use teams of experts in Delphi-type settings can enable rapid analysis and distinct consensus making (Hall, 2009a).

But in the case of something like the Gulf oil spill, it seems that the industry and industry association may be the best way to address this type of disaster (Coombs, 2010). The issues, resources and expertise is transnational and across a wide range of organizations.

Conclusions

BP, its business partners, the regulatory arm of the US Government, and the industry associations all performed poorly for the Great Gulf Spill to occur. Scenario planning could have, and should have been done in more depth in order to address issues of safety to strengthen disaster recovery plans. Once the event happened, BP and governments needed to quickly develop a Survival Plan. The company in the center of the fire—like BP in the gulf—should not be trying to manage the deluge of ideas while trying to manage the crisis; this will likely result in a lost opportunity for innovation.

One of the missed opportunities of BP recovery planning is the use of crowds and of experts, maybe something like what was developed for Katrina. The wisdom of crowds and the ability to use experts for adaptation and for innovation should not be underestimated. The tools should be employed in many ways, but there is no longer a reason why the implementation of them should take weeks or months. The ability to implement such a collaborative system for major events or major disasters could be done by governments, for-profit organizations (such as InnoCentive) or not-for-profits (such as the Gates Foundation). The Wikipedia paradigm, where crowds can be effectively employed to build millions of man-years worth of content in a matter of months, is something that bears more thought and development. The opportunity for innovation in the Gulf oil spill was a collateral casualty of the disaster, and so too may be many solutions for the next oil spill.

References

Alexa.com. (n.d.). *Top 500 global sites.* Retrieved from: www.alexa.com/top sites

Alexander, C. (2008). *The long tail: Why the future of business is selling less of more* (Rev. and updated ed.). New York, NY: Hyperion.

Anderson, L. D. W. (2010). This ain't your grandma's future: Tools to forecast technological innovations and strategies. In C.A. Lentz (Ed.), *The refractive thinker: Vol V: Strategy in innovation* (1st ed., pp. 31–51). Las Vegas, NV: The Lentz Leadership Institute.

Associated Press (AP). (2010, June 9). *BP's spill contingency plans vastly inadequate: Associated Press review of 582-page regional spill plan from 2009 shows dramatic shortcomings, poor research.* Retrieved from: www.cbsnews.com/stories/2010/06/09/national/main6563631.shtml/

Bentley, R., & Boyle, G. (2008). Global oil production: Forecasts and methodologies. *Environment & Planning B: Planning & Design, 35*(4), 609–626. doi:10.1068/b33063t.

BP, Plc. [BP]. (2010, September 8). *BP releases report on causes of Gulf of Mexico tragedy.* Retrieved from: www.bp.com/genericarticle.do?categoryId= 2012968&contentId=7064893

Cernansky, R. (2010, September 6). Will coal supplies peak in 2011? That's the prediction made by a recent study of reserves and historic coal production. *PlanetGreen.com* Retrieved from: http://planetgreen.discovery.com/work-connect/will-coal-supplies-peak-in-2011.html

Cheng, J. (2010, March 7). Most students use Wikipedia, avoid telling profs about it. *Ars Technica.* Retrieved from: http://arstechnica.com/science/news/2010/03/most-students-use-wikipedia-but-avoid-telling-profs-about-it.ars

Coombs, B. (2010, July 21). Four energy companies form oil spill reaction team. *CNBC.* Retrieved from: www.cnbc.com/id/38352657/Four_Energy_Companies_Form_Oil_Spill_Reaction_Team

DiPeso, J. (2005). Peak oil? *Environmental Quality Management, 15*(1), 111–118. doi:10.1002/tqem.20074.

Dye, R., Sibony, O., & Viguerie, S. P. (2009, April). Strategic planning: Three tips for 2009. *McKinsey Quarterly.* Retrieved from: www.mckinseyquarterly.com

Environmental Protection Agency (EPA). (2010). *National contingency plan.* Retrieved from: www.epa.gov/oem/docs/oil/edu/oilspill_book/chap7.pdf

Environmental Protection Agency [EPA]. (n.d.). *Climate change.* Retrieved from: www.epa.gov/climatechange/index.html

Friedman, T. (2009). *Hot, flat, and crowded: Why we need a green revolution—and how it can renew America.* New York, NY: Farrar, Straus, and Giroux.

Giles, J. (2005, December 15). Internet encyclopedias go head to head. *Nature. 438*(7070): 900–901. doi:10.1038/438900a

Gloor, P. A. (2005). *Swarm reactivity; Competitive advantage through collaborative innovation networks.* Oxford, UK: Oxford University Press.

Hall, E. (2009a). The Delphi primer: Doing real-world or academic research using a mixed-method approach. In C. A. Lentz (Ed.), *The refractive thinker: Vol. II. Research methodology* (pp. 3–26). Las Vegas, NV: The Lentz Leadership Institute.

Hall, E. (2009b). Strategic planning in times of extreme uncertainty. In C. A. Lentz (Ed.), *The refractive thinker: Vol. I. An anthology of higher learning* (1st ed., pp. 41–58). Las Vegas, NV: The Lentz Leadership Institute.

Hall, E. B. (2007). *Strategic economic development & marketing plan for Highlands County.* Morrisville, NC: LuLu Press. Retrieved from: http://Stores .LuLu.com/SBPlan

Hall, E. B., & Hinkelman, R. M. (2007). *Perpetual Innovation™: A guide to strategic planning, patent commercialization and enduring competitive advantage.* Morrisville, NC: LuLu Press.

Howe, J. (2009). *Crowdsourcing: Why the power of the crowd is driving the future of Business.* New York, NY: Three River Press.

Intergovernmental Panel on Climate Change [IPCC]. (2007). *Climate change 2007: Synthesis report,* (4th ed.). New York, NY: Cambridge University Press. Retrieved from: www.ipcc.ch/publications_and_data/publications_and_ data_reports.htm#1

Johnson, T. (2010, March 23). Healthcare costs and U.S. Competitiveness. *Council on Foreign Relations.* Retrieved from: www.cfr.org/publication/ 13325/healthcare_costs_and_us_competitiveness.html

Jordan, E. A. (2010). *The semiconductor industry and emerging technologies: A study using a modified Delphi Method.* (Doctoral dissertation). University of Phoenix, Phoenix, AZ.

Kaufmann, J. (2008, July 16). Peak oil: Causes and prospects. *Oregon Department of Energy. Model Steering Committee.* Retrieved from: www.oregon.gov/ODOT/TD/TPAU/docs/OMSC/PeakOil.pdf?ga=t

Kohli, R., & Melville, N. (2009). Learning to build an IT innovation platform. *Communications of the ACM, 52*(8), 122–126.

Kromm, C. (2010, June 4). Coal's dirty secret (a week-long series). *Institute of Southern Studies.* Retrieved from: www.southernstudies.org/2010/06/coals-dirty-secret-1.html

Libert, B., & Spector, J. (2009). *We are smarter than me: How to unleash the power of crowds in your business.* Upper Saddle River, NJ: Wharton School Publishing.

Lomborg, B. (2007). *The skeptical environmentalist: Measuring the real state of the world.* New York, NY: Cambridge University Press.

Mankiw, N. G. (2009). *Principles of economics* (5th ed.). New York, NY: Thomson/South-Western.

Mason, M. (2010, June 18). Rep. Joe Barton backs down from BP apology, 'shakedown' remark. *The Dallas Morning News.*

McKinsey Quarterly. (2009). Strategic and scenario planning. *McKinsey Quarterly.* Retrieved from www.McKinseyQuarterly.com

NcAdoo, T. (2009, October 14). How to cite Wikipedia in APA style. *APAStyle.org.* Retrieved from: http://blog.apastyle.org/apastyle/2009/10/how-to-cite-wikipedia-in-apa-style.html

Plato. (c. 380 BC). *The republic.* Athens. (427 BC - 347 BC).

Poister, T., & Thomas, J. (2007). The wisdom of crowds: Learning from administrators' predictions of citizen perceptions. *Public Administration Review, 67*(2), 279–289. doi:10.1111/j.1540–6210.2007.00713.x

Power, S. (2010, June 15). Shell, Exxon, Chevron and Conoco no better prepared to deal with a major oil spill than BP. *Wall Street Journal.*

Power, S., Kell, J., & Hughes, S. (2010, June 16). BP, oil industry take fire at hearing: Scientists raise estimate of leak to up to 60,000 barrels a day, raising fresh questions about containment plans. *Wall Street Journal.* Retrieved from: http://online.wsj.com/article/SB100014240527487040009804575308552817952036.html?mod=WSJ_latestheadlines

Reyes, R. (2010, June 18). BP receives more than 60,000 ideas to contain oil spill. *The Tampa Tribune.* Retrieved from http://www2.tbo.com/content/2010/jun/18/bp-receives-more-60000-ideas-contain-oil-spill/

Roger, H. (n.d). Peak oil and strategic resource wars: When the oil fields run dry—and they will—what will happen to the economies of petroleum producers? And what will that mean for the rest of us? The time to consider the potential scenarios and strategies is now. *The Futurist, 43*(5), 18.

Sawyer, K. (2007). *Group genius: The creative power of collaboration.* Kindle Digital Services.

Schwartz, P. (1996). *The art of the long view.* New York, NY: Doubleday.

Snyder, J. (2010, June 18). Markey will demand oil companies rewrite spill-response plans. *Business Week.* Retrieved from: www.businessweek.com/news/2010–06–18/markey-will-demand-oil-companies-rewrite-spill-response-plans.html

Stratopoulos, T., & Jee-Hae, L. (2010). IT innovation persistence: An oxymoron? *Communications of the ACM, 53*(5), 142–146.

Straus, S. G., Parker, A. M., Bruce, J. B., & Dembosky, J. W. (2009, April). *The group matters: A review of the effects of group interaction on processes and outcomes in analytic team.* Santa Monica, CA: RAND, National Security Research Division (Document No: WR-580-USG). Retrieved from: http://www.Rand.org

Surowiecki, J. (2005). *The wisdom of crowds: Why the many are smarter than the few and how collective wisdom shapes business, economies, societies and nations.* New York: NY: Anchor Books.

The United Nations Framework Convention on climate change [UNFCCC]. (n.d.). *Kyoto Protocol.* Retrieved from: http://unfccc.int/kyoto_protocol/items/2830.php

Walker, A. (2010, June 23). BP to InnoCentive: Sorry, we don't want your 908 ideas for saving the Gulf. *FastCompany.com.* Retrieved from: http://www.fastcompany.com/1663156/bp-to-innocentive-sorry-we-dont-want-your-908-ideas-for-saving-the-gulf

Walker, D. M. (2010). *Comeback America: Turning the country around and restoring fiscal responsibility.* New York, NY: Random House.

Wikipedia Foundation, Inc. [WF]. (2010, September 9). *Wikipedia, the free encyclopedia.* Retrieved from: http://en.wikipedia.org

Group Collaboration Using Wikipedia

This article makes extensive use of Wikipedia as a source and Table 1 demonstrates the quality of information used for each topic. No single page, i.e., article, had gone longer than 25 days since it was last updated. On average the articles were updated within 5 days! A spectacular feat, since the changes are reviewed by volunteer editors, before they are accepted. Edits that are not well documented are sometimes allowed but published with editorial comments and request for anyone reading the article to improve. Anyone can request a page be deleted, edit it, or contest it. In fact, some of the topics did not even exist prior to 2010. With 16 million pages (3.3 million in English), Wikipedia has many times more pages than other encyclopedias (WF, 2010, Encyclopedia). It is published in more than 100 languages, with surprising accuracy, and exceptional currency (WF, 2010, Wikipedia). An article in the magazine *Nature* suggested a rather high level of accuracy compared to Encyclopedia Britannica, finding 162 mistakes in the world's largest wiki compared to 123 in Britannica for a specific number of articles in each (WF, 2010, Encyclopedia, Wikipedia; Giles, 2005). Although Britannica complained about the methodology, *Nature* has not retracted the findings (WF, 2010, Encyclopedia). Just like an encyclopedia, "Wikipedia should be the first source of information, not the last" (Alexander, 2008, p. 69).

Wikipedia has matured to a reliable source of information to the point that businesses and academia must reevaluate their prejudices against using Wikipedia as a source. Thousands of volunteers review changes, indicate where citations are needed, flag sections that appear to have bias issues, and highlight sections that are contested. Citation notes, references, and external links are usually thorough for articles that are free of editor comments. The topics covered in Table 1 had approximately an average of 50 citations, called notes, with many articles having more than 200 notes. None of the articles were unfinished "stub" pages.

Wikipedia is one of the top destination for content in the world, consistently ranked in the top 10 web sited by Alexia.com (n.d.) worldwide and in the US (with at least half of those listed being search engines like Google and Yahoo, not actual destinations). Wikipedia competes with Facebook and YouTube as top content sites. Within Wikipedia, the top search terms in 2009 were "wiki" as #1 and Wikipedia as #5 (WF, 2010, Wikipedia); however, by September 2010 they had dropped to #9 and #31, respectively.

One of the astounding observations that can be seen from the 31 article topics in Table 1 is how amazingly *current* they are. The very nature of a wiki allows for rapid updates. Many topics would not even be included in an encyclopedia. There were no articles that had not been updated within the last 25 days of the day that the table was created. The average for days-since-last-updated was less than 5 days, the median was half of that and the mode was 0.

Companies have a special need to pay close attention to Wikipedia: where most companies may find that the first search results, after their own web site(s), will come from Wikipedia (Howe, 2009). Past customers will probably write updates and, if those customers were disgruntled, the article may be less-than flattering. Whatever is written will likely be supported by facts. Along with Wikipedia, companies need to monitor and manage all media and social media sites.

Academia had generally shunned Wikipedia as an unreliable source for formal research (McAddoo, 2009). One of the reasons is because the anonymous nature of Wikipedia edits does not indicate who wrote or who edited an article. Since anyone, anywhere, with any qualifications can post to a wiki; the reliability of all wikis has been in question. The question is, where does a researcher get good, reliable information about something that is *current*? Certainly not from a regular encyclopedia or from peer review journals? Wikipedia is often current within hours. General web searches will result in a bias from the profitability interests that pay to work themselves to the top results. Wikipedia is at the top of the destination and search results because it is relevant to the masses. The volume of participants is able to take back control of the Internet, where large money interests would typically control.

Wikipedia is an exceptional starting place for research. The researcher could certainly go read all of the relevant sources and avoid citing Wikipedia. Why is the use of an encyclopedia permitted, though? The 2005 *Nature* magazine showed the quality of Wikipedia; at the time Wikipedia was a relative infant that was just starting to walk; it will be 10 years old in 2011.

At the time of this research in September 2010, new metrics were available at Wikipedia that showed page views per month, internal article ranking, and the number of people watching each article/topic as shown in Table 1. May 2010 was the most recent month without missing data for each day of the month. Most pages had more than 1,000 views per month, representing a *lot* of people who can easily complain or correct if the information is incorrect. The watchers, however, may be the best indicator of quality control. There was an average of about 425 watchers (excluding categories without watcher information), so there are a lot of people watching the moment an edit occurs on almost any topic.

Academia needs to revisit Wikipedia. Professors are starting to

Category	PageViews May-10	Wiki Rank	Days Since Last Update	Improve Needed?	Cite/Notes	Approximate Number of:					Most Reliable Sources
						Watchers	Xlinks	Sources	Magazines	Peer Review	
encyclopedia	193,561	2,968	8	Some	29	424	~40	~40	few	some	Articles and encyclopedia companies themselves
innovation	70,350	7,530	5		23	149	~100	~100	many	many	USPTO.gov;WIPO.int; other countries PTOs
invention	21,960		5		32	90	~100	~100	many	many	USPTO.gov;WIPO.int; other countries PTOs
patent	72,970	8,186	5		40	211	~100	~100	many	many	USPTO.gov;WIPO.int: other countries PTOs
TRIZ	9,050	90	10	Sources	couple	-	several	several	few	few	Genrich Altshuller's books and TRIZ Journals
Delphi Method	16,263		0		8	48	~20	~20	several	several	RAND
scenario planning	9,933		5	Some	29	38	~50	~50	several	several	Schwarz book, etc.
disaster recovery plan (DRP)	733		5	Some*	4	72	~20	~30	several	few	ANSI, ISO, BSI, etc. (See BCP)
business continuity planning (BCP)	21,999		3		5	80	~50	~40	several	several	ANSI, ISO, BSI, etc. (See DRp)
collaborative innovation network	1,128		6	Some	~few	-	~10	~20	few	few	Gloor & companies information
groupware	3,638		10	Some	8	-	~50	~50	several	few	IBM, User groups & Companies' information
collaborative software	22,133		1		couple	107	~100	~100	no	no	Comparison of companies products
cloud computing / SaaS	316,621	336	0		113	394	~100	~100	many	few	Magazines & Research firms
social network service	89,839	8,508	0		65	437	~100	~100	many	some	Magazines & Research firms
wisdom of crowds	1,787		1	Some	8	-	~20	~20	few	few	Surowiecki & others
global warming	463,499	72	2		132	1,488	100+	50+	very many	very many	NASA's JPL; NOAA; IPCC; etc.
climate change	107,175	1,525	5		40	259	~80	~40	many	many	UN & Country governments (See global warming)
economic bubble	16,545		11		19	78	~30	~30	several	several	Government and news articles
Recession of 2008	1,206		1	Some	255	-	~100	~100	many	many	Government, news and peer articles
Deepwater Horizon oil spill	730,900		0	Edit	313	296	400+	~50	very many	very many	Government agencies and news
peak oil	60,980	9,267	0		198	198	~200	~150	many	few	UN & Country governments, associations, magazine, etc.
oil spills / largest oil spills	66,913		3		51	-	~100	~30	many	few	Government agencies and news
mining accidents	646		2		17	-	~50	~50	many	some	Government agencies and news
open source	89,153	6,718	0	Edit	44	334	~150	~50	many	few	Magazines & Articles & Research firms
Creative Commons Attribution	149		1	Edit	19	-	~20	~20	couple	none	Creative Commons; Creative Commons Int'l
Web 2.0 / Web 3.0	147,025	1,541	8	Some	54	1,093	~60	~60	several	few	Magazines & Research firms
Web conferencing	24,283		2		5	72	30+	30+	few	some	Companies' product information
wiki	2,937,803	9	0		29	1,941	30+	30+	few	few	Books and Articles
Wikipedia®	1,290,533	31	2		200+	3,335	100+	100+	many	several	Wikipedia Foundation
WikiBooks.org	17,616		25		15	88	30+	30+	several	several	Wikipedia Foundation
Wikiversity	16,541		15	Expand	15	59	30+	30+	several	several	Wikipedia Foundation

Table 1. *Wikipedia Articles, Citations and the Reliability of the Information*

integrate Wikipedia into their classes, by getting students to review, evaluate, and update what they find there ("Wikipedia for Credit", 2010). A recent study shows that three-fourths of students use Wikipedia and 30% *always* use it, even though they rarely cite it (Cheng, 2010). Students are well aware of the possible limitations. But students do not necessarily know what they should consider before using Wikipedia as a source. Since students are widely using it, guidelines should be developed to indicate when a Wikipedia article is acceptable. Considerations for an article should include how much it is being monitored, used, updated, and the number of reliable sources. If an article is flagged by the reviewers indicating that it needs citations or edits, it should probably not be used as a source.

About the Author

Dr. Elmer Hall holds several accredited degrees: a Bachelor of Arts (BA) and Master of Business Administration (MBA) from the University of South Florida; and a Doctorate of International Business Administration (DIBA) from Nova South-eastern University. Throughout his schooling, he was a management and research assistant involved in business/trade research and systems development. He has taught at the undergraduate and graduate levels (MBA and MIS) at several Florida universities and currently is a Professor of Business at Warner University where he teaches masters and undergraduate business classes and is the Interim Sustainability Officer. He also is a Facilitator and Dissertation Mentor for the University of Phoenix. His "real" education, however, is from his personal entrepreneurial ventures and those of his clients.

Dr. Elmer is the President and CEO of Strategic Business Planning Company, a company that does strategic planning workshops as well as consulting on the development of business plans, strategic information systems plans and intellectual property commercialization plans (www.SBPlan.com). He has been involved in strategic planning or systems development for hundreds of companies. Many of them were small ventures that he helped develop startup business plans; others were longer-term including consulting activities with IBM, Ryder, Florida Power & Light, and Burger King (Diageo).

With Robert 'Bob' M. Hinkelman, Dr. Elmer coauthored *Perpetual Innovation™: A Guide to Strategic Planning, Patent Commercialization and Enduring Competitive Advantage.* SBP has developed the Commercialization of Patent Assets, COMPASS®, process for intellectual property (IP) management (www.ipPlan.com).

To reach Dr. Elmer Hall, for information on any of these topics, please e-mail: elmer@SBPlan.com

This Ain't Your Grandma's Future: Tools to Forecast Technological Innovations and Strategies

Dr. Lois D. Wiley Anderson

In the early part of the 1970s, Alvin Toffler spoke about the world of tomorrow and provided the following advice in his book, *Future Shock.*

> Three hundred and fifty years after his death, scientists are still finding evidence to support Cervantes' succinct insight into adaptational psychology: "Forewarned fore-armed." Self-evident as it may seem, in most situations we can help individuals adapt better if we simply provide them with advance information about what lies ahead. (Toffler, 1971, p. 418)

Futurists use open and non-bias language techniques to define and discuss forecasting methodologies along with the power and purpose of each method. This article is just such a discussion of those techniques and methodologies. Leaders can make minor adjustments to tailor each of the methods and generate results with increased application to their particular organization.

Perhaps the most important adjustment of all is shifting the way one thinks about the fundamental changes in the future. Refractive thinkers are 'out of the box' or better yet, 'there is no box' thinkers. Refractive thinkers are challengers of constraints and conventions. Joel Barker (1992) provided the same sort of challenge in his work *Para-*

digms: The Business of Discovering the Future. Barker's landmark book identified customary boundaries and traditionally accepted behaviors as the source of paradigms that restrict the ability to forecast. The title of this article purposely and antagonistically addresses the need to change one's thinking. No, this *ain't* your grandma's future.

The future is becoming less predictable and the speed of technological change is increasing. Human being's ability to assess, plan, and prepare for the future must increase in speed and accuracy to match that of technological change. The ability to prepare for the technological future cannot rely solely upon methods such as traditional strategic planning which depends primarily upon the perceptions of organizational leaders. In fact, expert strategic planning consultants have long defined strategic planning as "the process by which the guiding members of an organization envision its future" (Goodstein, Nolan, & Pfeiffer, 1993, p. 3). Methods of planning and perceptions must not restrict the capacity to anticipate and plan for the future notwithstanding the normal bias held by leaders (Hall, 2009a; Hall & Hinkelman, 2007). As Toffler postulated over 30 years ago and Cervantes declared some 400 years past, the use of strategic planning will be better positioned, more accurate, and assist leaders of organizations and governments to meet the challenges of the future if there is some insight, some perception, and some understanding of what the future will bring. The informed insight does not have to be proof beyond a mathematical certainty; nor can it be. The insight does need to be more than the vision of a single leader or a small group of like-minded leaders who have biases based on their common experiences and historical perspectives.

Planning Methods to Inform Innovation and Future Strategies

There are methods of planning that can assist in visualizing the future which can overcome the limitations of traditional planning and open the minds of leaders to a more diverse range of possibilities. These methods allow the assessment of the future and a plan for greater varieties of occurrences; they include trend analysis, trend extrapolation, cross-impact analysis, Delphi method, and scenario development. This article includes definitions and discussions of each of these methodologies using real and hypothetical situations to enrich and clarify the reader's understanding of each methods' purpose and power for assessment in technology—assessment which will help leaders manage technology to improve the human condition (Brookmeyer, Johnson, Ziegler-Graham, & Arrighi, 2007; Ewing & Bartholomen, 2009; Katz, 2003; Narayanan & Zane, 2009; Sabo, 2009). The *problem is not* that these tools have not heretofore existed—because they did. None of these tools is new. The *problem is* that leaders have allowed bias and political correctness to interfere with their use of these tools and consequently they have failed to *read the tealeaves* of tomorrow. The framework used to inform leaders and free them to look into the future will find them better informed and thus better prepared to deal with the future technological innovations. No doubt—Cervantes would applaud these efforts.

Trend Analysis

Trend analysis is the simple act of looking for patterns. Trend Analysis looks for events that reoccur over time, as well as, observing the direction and intensity of those reoccurring events. The events can be as complicated as the emergence of new technologies over ten years or as simple as an average wind speed over the course of a day reported by a wind farm assessor, as demonstrated in Figure 1. In this example, the assessor observes the average wind speed increases throughout the day. The one-day observance is similar to the records kept by the wind farm operator. Therefore, the trend analysis seems to indicate that the wind farm operator has maintained valid records.

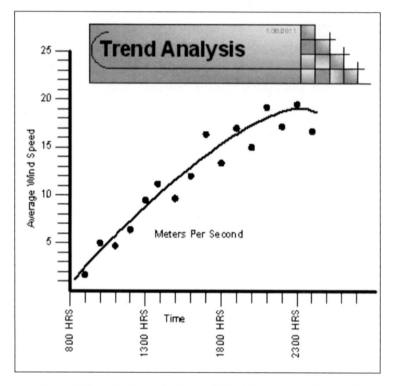

Figure 1: Sample Trend Analysis of Wind Speed at a 'low wind' Wind Turbine Installation © 2010 by L.D.W. Anderson

John Naisbitt produced *Megatrends: Ten New Directions Transforming Our Lives* in 1982. This book identified ten major trends from an economic, social, and cultural perspective. In 1990, Naisbitt and Aburdene, built upon Naisbitt's original work with the release of *Megatrends 2000: Ten New Directions for the 1990's.* Both *Megatrends* publications were the product of over ten years of analyzing articles from newspapers accumulated from selected cities around the

United States of America. From their research Naisbitt and Aburdene identified in both of the *Megatrends* books the development of biotechnology as a trend which has the potential to make "awesome contributions to the improvement of life, it also raises questions that make people uneasy" (1990, p. 259). Naisbitt did a statistical analysis of the frequency with which biotechnological articles and mentions of biotechnological advances appeared in nationwide newspapers. Using this body of information, he was able to chart the direction and the intensity of the observed data. The abundance of articles regarding the plans, use, and impacts of biotechnological application increased significantly in number and in frequency of occurrence over a given period, in this case the time span was 10 years. Based on the collected data, Naisbitt observed that biotechnology was an ever-increasing trend, which appeared to have an ever-increasing impact upon the human condition in terms of our culture, economy, and society.

In 2006, Naisbitt wrote *Mind Set* a work that defined the problem with leader's ability to use the data derived from trend analysis. Naisbitt used the term *mind set* and not *mindset,* for that reason, this article will follow the Naisbitt style. The mind sets tend to create biases and to lessen the negative impact of those mind sets, leaders must acknowledge the existence of the biased mind set. What follows are some, but not all of the mind sets identified by Naisbitt.

- "While many things change, most things remain the same" (Nasbitt, 2006, p. 3), this mind set speaks to the natural leveling of trends and the failure to give warranted attention to constants that remain unchanged.

- "Resistance to change falls if the benefits are real" (Nasbitt, 2006, p. 57), change management programs tend to focus on how to get people to accept change and yet if the people involved can see the benefits of the change the resistance will cease.

Perhaps the reason organizations experience so much resistance to change and resistance to analysis of the future is that benefits are not clear, management failed to provide a clear communication of the benefits, or the benefits do not exist. If there is a hidden agenda driving the change, employees may feel that the publicly expressed reasons for the change are a sham. Active and passive-aggressive resistance to change is likely to increase when people do not believe the stated reasons for change. Other mind sets are,

- "The future is embedded in the present" (Nasbitt, 2006, p. 11), this is the essence of trend analysis;

- "Understanding how powerful it is not to have to be right" (Nasbitt, 2006, p. 33), is a major paradigm shift for most leaders.

Yet this mind set that one cannot fail or must be right, might have kept post-it notes from reaching the market, as they resulted from an adhesive failure. For purposes of specific technological assessment, Naisbitt offers this mind set: "Don't forget the ecology of technology" (Nasbitt, 2006, p. 99). Included in the ecology of technology is the use of human beings to perform hands-on work and the importance that technology adoption is not measured in a vacuum without consideration of the existing organizational environment.

Some people tend to embrace new technology as if the newness creates a need and all new technology is good. Biotechnology has lead to many ethical concerns (i.e. destruction of human embryonic cells). Naisbitt frames the importance of looking at both the potential good and bad of technology when he states, "Technology is on the fork of blessing and plague, and again, very few examine it" (Nasbitt, 2006, p. 104).

Technology replacing human jobs is an embedded part of the next mind set.

- "DON'T FORGET THE ECOLOGY OF TECHNOLOGY in most companies, human scale was set aside during the industrial era. We are now returning to it" (Nasbitt, 2006, p. 107).

Naisbitt points to the emergence of China as a world producer and the use of humans versus technology. The analysis to technology must not be from just the perspective of usefulness, but also from many other directions such as economic, political, and environmental.

If trend analysis is to be a valuable tool, leaders must open their minds to many possibilities and acknowledge the bias created by mind sets. Those people using trend analysis must deliberately develop mind sets that unlock the mind to embrace change and limitless possibilities. With a mind free to explore the potential, trend analysis is improved and is even more powerful in that it provides a clear means for researchers to describe how the past became the present.

Trend Extrapolation

Having reviewed the elements of trend analysis the next step toward a more complete technological assessment is trend extrapolation. "Trend extrapolation is the projecting or forecasting of a trend into the future" (Sterry & Hendricks, 1997, p. 128). Trend extrapolation is the logical extension of trend analysis to perform a trend extrapolation; one must first have collected the data to create a trend analysis. With a trend analysis in place, one can project the observable trends into the future using tools such as forecast function, trendline, or line-of-best-fit. These statistical tools are available in spreadsheet programs. Note that a trend extrapolation does not predict the future; it merely projects what may happen as informed by the intensity and direction of the trend. Many factors may alter the direction and intensity of a trend; Sterry and Hendricks (1997) identify these factors as *forcing factors* (p. 129). Catastrophic events involving traditional carbon-based fuels tend to alter the public's acceptance or resistance to alternative sources of energy significantly. Such forcing factors include, but are not limited to events such as the 1986 Chernobyl reactor meltdown, 1989 Exxon Valdez oil spill, and in 2010 the BP Gulf of Mexico Spill (Alaska Oil Spill Commission, 2009; U.S. DOE, 2010; U.S. NRC, 2009). As seen in Figure 2, a trend extrapolated in concert with other events seems to indicate a public reaction to increased awareness of energy use. In the period from 1986 to 1992, there was a down turn in the consumption of electricity in the U.S. One could extrapolate that Chernobyl and the Exxon Valdez accidents increased public awareness of energy use. The increased awareness resulted in greater attention to energy use and thus a reduction in the use of electricity.

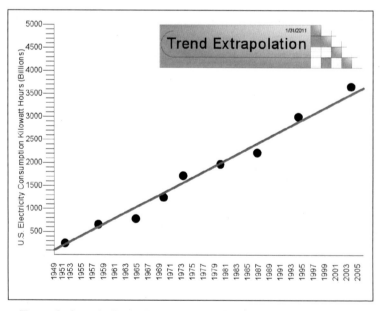

Figure 2: Sample Trend Extrapolation of U.S. Energy Consumption
© 2010 by L.D.W. Anderson

Management firms wishing to project data for expansion, product development, potential product failures, machine maintenance, worker availability, insurance losses, and so forth might do well to use trend extrapolation. As an example, a manufacturing firm might receive a shipment of component parts that prove to have a very high failure rate in the field. Several department managers would be interested to know the following; how any service calls are likely to result from this problem; is there a seasonal trend to the failures; and what is the anticipated financial charge-back to the supplier? These are only a few of the questions for which a trend extrapolation will prove an excellent tool.

To perform the trend extrapolation in this hypothetical manufacturing situation, the following steps are required:

1. Collect data on the number of affected parts received from shipment records.

2. Collect failure data from the warranty department.

3. Collect *first-item* check data from the quality department. (In quality assurance terms the *first-item* or *first-article* check is a standard quality test performed on incoming product shipments.)

4. Compare the number of known failures with the total number of parts shipped.

5. Analyze the observable trend in the failure data.

6. Account for deviations in the trend, such as seasonally higher product usage, cold-, or heat-induced failures due to weather and geographical location, and so forth.

7. Select an appropriate statistical tool based upon the observable trend (i.e. a linear line of best-fit would not be an appropriate choice because the problem will not go on to infinity. There are a finite number of component parts involved. In all probability, the

quality data would reveal that the failure rate would be unlikely to reach one-hundred percent. There may tend to be multiple variables such as a consistent trend with seasonal impacts, an upward trend with seasonal impacts, and so forth. One method of statistical analysis does not fit all data.)

8. Perform the selected statistical operation on the data, based upon the known failures. One may improve the validity of the analysis to use two different operations and compare the results.

9. Review and evaluate the results of the extrapolation.

Once these steps are complete, the department managers in this hypothetical manufacturing firm have a specific body of data arranged in a descriptive form. Managers must give attention to persons or events that could alter the neutrality of the data collection. Avoid intentional or unintentional alteration of the raw data. If employees concerned about job effects alter any of the data used for the extrapolation, the trend extrapolation will not produce meaningful results; take care to insure the integrity of the historical data. Some individuals may be concerned that the data collection is a means to place blame. The purpose of the data collection and compilation must be clear to all departments involved. The desired outcome of this procedure is to find the root problem and avoid further problems. This compiled and unaltered data extrapolated to the future provides a foundation for informed and logical decision-making. The situational data presented as a solid foundation of information projected to the future increases the likelihood that future decision will be more accurate, that is the power of trend extrapolation.

Cross-Impact Analysis (CIA)

If the information analyzed is composed of a set of random or multi-attribute measures, the data does not fit a trend analysis or trend extrapolation. Cross-impact analysis is an assessment tool for use when there are a variety of uncertainties. One might liken CIA to a line of falling dominos. When the first domino is gently pushed, the result is that as that domino falls against the next domino, that falling domino affects the next and so forth. Sterry and Hendricks (1997) describe CIA as ". . . a research tool that is used to show the relationship between two trends or events" (p. 129).

One might look at the proliferation of computers for an example of CIA. As computers became the standard method of processing words, it was widely touted that we were quickly moving toward a 'paperless' society. Due to the resistance of human beings to read only from a computer screen, we are using more and more paper as readers, in particular students, print the e-books (Par, 2010; Stabo, 2009). Sandler, Armstrong, and Nardini (2007) explained resistance by readers to e-book products. In the "the sluggish uptake of e-books is not only about product development, but the development of the market that ultimately needs to accept it" (2007, para. 2). The increased use of paper resulting from increased computer usage may seem counter-intuitive. If one looks at the interrelated trends of *computer usage* and *electronic information availability,* a cross-impact emerges. Computer usage has increased to the point, in the USA, that over 68% of all homes have a computer (NTIA, 2009). There is more electronic information available today than ever before and the availability of additional information is increasing exponentially. The most current albeit unofficial estimates are that one can locate more than 29 billion pages of information on the Internet. These demographics provoke an unspecified number of interesting quandaries. If 68% of our homes have computers, then over 30% of our homes do not have computers (NTIA, 2009). How is one to exchange information with the computer have-nots? If more people are interested in additional information stored electronically and yet there are scores of people who do not have home computers, many people must increase the amount of printing to share the stored knowledge. Today the unemployment rates around the world are soaring to new heights. At the same time, the use of computers to file for unemployment and other services is increasing. Many of the people using a computer to file for benefits are going to workforce centers or their local libraries. In Indiana, North Dakota, and many other states, the initial unemployment benefit forms must be completed online (Job Search North Dakota, 2006; Pierce County Library System, n.d.a; Pierce County Library System, n.d.b.). Since the filer is not on a private computer if he or she is to retain proof of filing for unemployment, the form must be printed rather than saved electronically (Carey, 2002; Collett, 2010; Gritsch, 2009; Tharp, 2009). To have a record of their filing and proof of compliance they must print at least copies of the confirmation pages. Some unemployed persons may wish to print instructions, timelines, government announcements, and other parts of the unemployment insurance site. This is just one example of computer usage resulting in increases in the use of paper. The production of paper, which reflects the use of paper, has grown steadily in EU countries at an annual rate of 2.5% since the 2000 (EU, 2009; Sweeney & Lynch, 2010).

There is a revolution in the offerings of electronic publications (i.e. textbooks, magazines, research journals, novels and more). If the document readers (i.e. Kindle®, iPad®, and so forth) have not advanced to the point where ease of transportability for a majority of the population is as constrained by the coast and the reader units have not become as inexpensive as a paperback book, does that not result in more material being printed? The list goes on with more questions leading to more questions. Just like the dominos, one impact results in an equal and opposite impact. If one domino falls against two staggered rows of dominos, the impact creates falling rows in two directions at the same time. Millett and Zelman illustrate the Cross-Impact Analysis in the form of a logic model in their 2005 article that supported the use of scenario analysis for the Ohio Department of Education.

Figure 3 shows one method of illustrating a Cross Impact Analysis. The topic used for this demonstration is the selection of a Wind Farm site to generate electricity. The first step was for the researcher to identify the six main areas of concern. A review of each major area considers the impact it can have on the other five topics. Land for access roads has the potential for contentious relations with local citizens. The local government could acquire land using Public

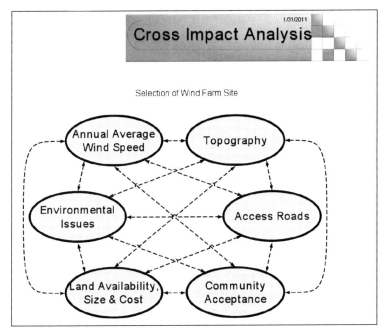

Figure 3: Sample Cross Impact Analysis for Selection of Wind Farm Site © 2010 by L.D.W. Anderson

Domain. Wind Farm management could purchase land. This is just one brief part of the cross impact analysis and just one manner to format the data analysis. Another common way to present cross impact analysis is via a matrix and with the importance of each main area assigned a numeric rating. The most important facet of the Cross Impact Analysis is the 360-review of the forecasted issue studied.

Cross-Impact Analysis is a tool, which has been used by many to look at technological developments in a linear (impact to impact), and yet non-linear manner (multiple impacts upon multiple impacts). The power of using CIA is the ability to deal with multiple impacts branching in multiple directions (DeSmet, Springael, & Kunsch, 2002; Keisler, 2002; Lee & Kim, 2010).

The Delphi Method

For more than 50 years, a multiplicity of Delphi and Delphi-like studies forecasted military plans, strategies, potential enemy actions, commercial innovations, and any type of forecasting from which expert-informed opinion can benefit (Grisham, 2009; Gritsch, 2009; Martino, 1972; Sackman, 1974). Olaf Helmer and Norman Dalkey are the fathers of the Delphi method of research. Helmer and Dalkey of the RAND Corporation developed the Delphi Method in 1953. Experts use informed judgment in responding to questionnaires (Brown, 1968). There are three distinctive characteristics in the Delphi research procedure, they are: "(1) anonymity, (2) controlled feedback, and (3) statistical group response" (Dalkey, 1967, p. 3). Participants involved in the Delphi consider and reconsider their responses in light of a given set of opinions of other participants as the rounds of the Delphi proceed. Brown (1968) wrote:

Delphi replaces direct confrontation and debate by a carefully planned, orderly program of sequential individual interroga-

tions . . . [and it] . . . attempts to improve the panel or committee approach by subjecting the views of individual experts
to each other's criticism in ways that avoid face to face confrontation and provide anonymity of opinion and arguments
advanced in defense of those opinions. (p. 3)

Given the lack of direct confrontation and preservation of confi-
dentiality, the Delphi is much like a secret ballot that leads itself to
honest and open responses from all participants. Those in a position
of power have no more impact on the outcome of the Delphi than
does the lowest ranking member of the expert panel. The forecast
resulting from a Delphi is a powerful tool for strategic management
and projecting technological innovations.

In general, a Delphi yields more than a technological forecast,
since the technique creates within itself the perceived wants or needs
of respondents. The method replaces a direct face-to-face dialogue
by a carefully designed program of anonymous individual opinion
polls (DuBois, & Dueker, 2009; Helmer, 1967). Sequentially an
interjection of information and views of the participants complete
the idea generation process. The Delphi Method is best suited to
gain a consensus on a topic without having to conduct a face-to-face
meeting (Anderson, 2000; Croft, 2007; Hall, 2009b). In this process
of forecasting, the researcher attempts to predict what can happen
instead of what will happen (Dalkey, 1969).

The Delphi Method has been most successful for forecasting purposes (Brockhouse & Mickelsen, 1977; Gordon, 1968). Brockhouse
and Mickelsen's (1977) analysis of 598 Delphi studies found 26% in
the physical sciences and engineering, 23% in business and economics, 23% in social sciences, 19% in biological sciences and medicine,
and 19% in education and public administration. For purposes of
illustrating the basic flow of a Delphi, Figure 4 shows a study that
took seven rounds to reach consensus. The Delphi Method does not

specify a number of rounds. The classic Delphi rounds continue until the expert panel achieves consensus. Researchers frequently use a Modified-Delphi and limit the number of rounds conducted. The researcher combines like results into categories of broadly equivalent statements to facilitate the limited rounds model.

One major advantage of the Delphi study is the lower cost involved. Panel members reduce costs by not meeting together physically (Sackman, 1974). Panel members are also able to experience independent and rational thought and intimidated by the ideas of the others because they never meet face-to-face (Brockhouse & Mick-

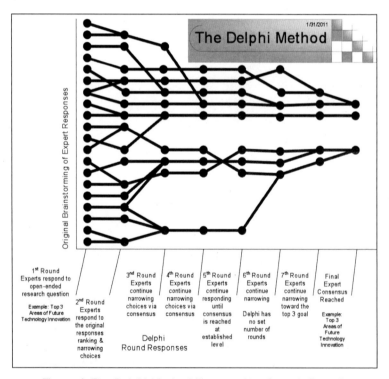

Figure 4: The Delphi Method Illustrated as Generic Rounds
© 2010 by L.D.W. Anderson

elsen, 1977; Brownlie, 2009). Finally, yet importantly, most Delphi studies take a relatively short period to complete (Sackman, 1974).

Researchers considering using the Delphi Method must also be aware that Bramson and Paulette have identified numerous disadvantages and limitations of the Delphi Method (as cited in Delbecq, Van de Ven, & Gustafson, 1975). Those negatives are:

1. The panelist can become fatigued after several rounds. This condition may affect the quality of their input.

2. The quality of a Delphi study is heavily dependent upon the selection of a proper panel of experts. Shortcomings in their area of expertise can cast doubt on the value of the study's results.

3. Several months may be required to complete a full Delphi study.

4. Except for the justification of dissenting opinions, Delphi does not offer any means to know why one selected one response over another.

5. Administration of a Delphi study may be complex and time consuming.

6. Communication problems, if they occur, may be difficult to resolve.

7. Experimental support related to the validly and reliability of the method does not currently exist.

Performing a Modified Delphi that limits the number of rounds overcomes the major limitation of the traditional Delphi. In addition to limiting the number of rounds, another modification could be to provide space for a panelist to provide a written justification for his or her response. The use of a website to collect data and disseminate the findings from previous rounds can shorten the time needed to conduct a Delphi and may reduce fatigue factor of panelists.

Scenario Development

All of the previously discussed forecasting methods used collected data or previously existing knowledge to inform the researcher. When the researcher has only a vision of a potential future, another type of forecasting method is used and that is the creation of an imagined sequence of events or circumstances. Scenario development is simply put—creating stories. Figure 5 illustrates a systematic approach to creating a viable scenario. The stories and the process of creating them advances the understanding about the future and the possibilities one may encounter. Methodically planning and creating scenarios allows an analysis that supports efforts to be proactive in dealing with the ambiguity of future events (Forge, 2009; Gilliland & Guseman, 2009; Perrottet, 1996). Creating scenarios should be an interactive process, which encourages countless insights and substantial plans to manage the future use and implementation of technologies. Willmore (1998) suggests the following system to develop a useful futures scenario.

Step 1: Articulate the Business Idea

Step 2: Define the Focus and Scope

Step 3: Identify Trends

Step 4: Identify Key Themes

Step 5: Create a Scenario Matrix

Step 6: Refine the Scenarios

Step 7: Identify Insights

Step 8: Formalize Lessons Learned (pp. 2–10)

Willmore (1998) used a process for developing scenarios that is similar to one proposed by Caldwell (1999), a Professor Emeritus,

Soil, Water, and Environmental Science at the University of Arizona in his site titled *Anticipating the Future: Focus on Environment.* Caldwell presents a web page as part of the course labeled *Seminar of Futures Techniques* where he simplified the scenario development process into just three steps (1999). Caldwell's succinct list of steps to create scenarios includes: 1) identify driving forces, 2) describe realistic trends, and 3) group trends into several different scenarios asking *what if* questions about those scenarios. Caldwell's materials are housed on the University of Arizona servers (http://ag.arizona.edu/futures/fut/semtech).

The South African government used scenario development in 1991 and 1992 to assess the major changes in their societal situation and to assess the future of South African society. The scenarios take their name from the Mont Fleur Conference Center near Cape Town where the development workshop took place. There were 22 participants in the scenario development workshop including representations of academia, business, government, and political activists. According to the facilitator for the Mont Fleur scenario project, Adam Kahan, "The purpose of Mont Fleur was not to present definite truths, but to stimulate debate on how to shape the next 10 years" (Kahan, 1999, p. 1). Although the Mont Fleur scenarios did not solve the societal problems of the ending of apartheid, they did serve to shift the opinion of workshop participants closer to middle ground, thereby helping the *conflicting groups* work together to reach the consensus needed to build a new and better society in South Africa. The Mont Fleur Scenarios exemplify the best use of scenario development.

Scenarios are stories, they are creative writing, but they are not science fiction. The process or incremental steps to creating scenarios use facts and plausible outcomes. No matter the steps used to produce the scenarios, the power of scenario development comes from the ability to describe several possible outcomes and generate informed discussion about those outcomes (Clemens, 2009).

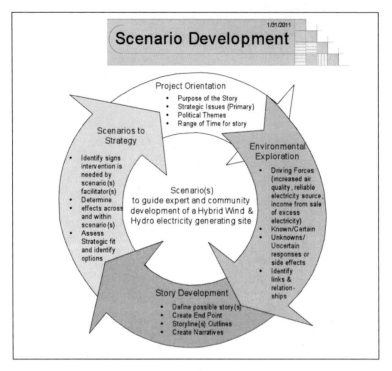

Figure 5: Sample Scenario Development for Development of a Hydro-Wind Hybrid Development © 2010 by L.D.W. Anderson

Conclusion

The methods which were discussed here, (trend analysis, trend extrapolation, cross-impact analysis, Delphi method, and scenario development) can improve the ability to assess the future and to be better prepared to deal with the complications of that future. The tools are not new, but with the minor alternations suggested and by combining their usage, forecasting the future can be better than ever before. Throwing off the limitations and a restrictive vision of the future will create an environment where forecasting tools are used to their fullest advantage.

A major future complication will be simply dealing with the never-ending occurrences in everyday life. In the 1950s, the wristwatch-video-phone worn by Dick Tracy in the Sunday Cartoon section of the newspaper was science fiction, but today it is science fact. Today the newspaper industry has nearly collapsed under the weight of electronic and instant delivery of the news. Each new technological development replaces what was new just yesterday (Tapscott & Williams, 2006). The very nature of human beings is an innate curiosity and understanding that to one degree or another—reality is changing daily. Human beings must be ready and willing to deal with change and to evaluate the technology driving that change. Joseph Schumpeter's (1975) idea of creative destruction contends that it is not viable to generate something appreciably innovative without completely shifting or destroying, what came before. Creative destruction is an excellent way to describe our technological future. The architect has a blueprint—a plan for the new construction, one might even say—a guide to the future. The community accepts the plan for development and change. The construction demolition expert systematically brings down the old structure to build the framework for a new architectural achievement. The futurist tools are like the architects' plans—they help us embrace or reject new technological advances. The systematic assessment of technology will better prepare us for the future and the creative destruction that innovation can leave in its wake. Cervantes' perceptions regarding human beings' ability to adapt to change still holds true—those forewarned are fore armed.

End Note: The graphics created for this article are not from real situations. Each of these samples is only one of the possible ways to present these forecasting tools and the associated data.

References

Alaska Oil Spill Commission. (1990, February). *Spill: The wreck of the Exxon Valdez*. Final Report, Author. Available electronically at http://www.evostc.state.ak.us

Anderson, L. D. W. (2000). *Survival competencies required of human resource development generalists who are solo-performers in organizations in the next five years: A modified-Delphi study*. (Doctoral Dissertation). Available from Pro-Quest Dissertations and Theses database. (UMI No. 731887151)

Barker, J. A. (1993). Paradigms: The business of discovering the future. New York, NY: Harper Business.

Brockhouse, W. L., & Mickelsen, J. F. (1977). An analysis of prior Delphi applications and some observations on its future applicability. *Technological Forecasting and Social Change, 10(1)*, pp. 103–110.

Brookmeyer, R., Johnson, E., Ziegler-Graham, K., & Arrighi, H. M. (2007). Forecasting the global burden of Alzheimer's disease. Alzheimer's and Dementia *3*(3), 186–191. Retrieved from http://works.bepress.com/rbrookmeyer/23

Brown, B. (1968, September). Delphi process: A methodology used for the elicitation of opinions of experts (Report #P-3925). Santa Monica, CA: The RAND Corporation.

Brownlie, D. (2009). Tales of prospects past: On strategic fallacies and uncertainty in technology forecasting. *Journal of Marketing Management, 25*(5/6), 401.

Caldwell, R. L. (1999). Anticipating the future: Focus on environment. *Seminar of futures techniques*. University of Arizona. Available electronically at http://ag.arizona.edu/futures/fut/semtech

Carey, T. W. (2002, November). The electronic investor: Eliminating your paper trail. *Barron's, 82(45)*, T6.

Clemens, R. (2009). Environmental scanning and scenario planning: A 12 month perspective on applying the viable system model to developing public sector foresight. *Systemic Practice and Action Research, 22*(4), 249–274.

Collett, S. (2010, January). Taming the printer chaos. *Computerworld, 44(2)*, 26–28.

Croft, J. (2007, August). Conflict: Crime and war compared. *The RUSI Journal, 152(4),* 40–45.

Dalkey, N. C. (1967, October). *Delphi.* (Report #P-3704). Santa Monica, CA: The RAND Corporation.

Dalkey, N. C. (1969, June). *The Delphi method: An experimental study of group opinion.* (Report #RM-5888-PR). Santa Monica, CA: The RAND Corporation.

Delbecq, A. L., Van de Ven, A. H., & Gustafson, D. H. (1975). *Group techniques for program planning.* Glenview, IL: Scott, Foresman and Co.

DeSmet, Y., Springael, J., & Kunsch, P. (2002). Towards statistical multicriteria decision modeling: A first approach. *Journal of Multicriteria Decision Analysis, 11*(6), 305–313.

DuBois, J., & Dueker, J. (2009). Teaching and assessing the responsible conduct of research: A Delphi consensus panel report. *Journal of Research Administration, 40*(1), 49–70.

European Union (EU). (2009, May). Directive 2009/28/EC of the European Parliament and of the Council of 23 April 2009 on the promotion of the use of energy from renewable sources and amending and subsequently repealing directives 2001/77/EC and 2003/30/3c. *Official Journal of the European Union.* 5.6.2009, 59(140), 16–61.

Ewing, R., & Bartholomew, K. (2009). Comparing land use forecasting methods: Expert panel versus spatial interaction model. American Planning Association. *Journal of American Planning Association, 75*(3), 343–357.

Forge, S. (2009). Forecasting quantitatively using micro/meso/macro-economics with scenarios for qualitative balance. Foresight: *The Journal of Futures Studies. Strategic Thinking and Policy, 11*(1), 43–60.

Gilliland, M., & Guseman, S. (2009). Forecasting new products by structured analogy. *The Journal of Business Forecasting, 28*(4), 12–15.

Goodstein, L., Nolan, T., & Pfeiffer, J. W. (1993). *Applied strategic planning: How to develop a plan that really works.* New York, NY: McGraw-Hill, Inc.

Gordon, P. (1968). *Principles of phase Diagrams in materials systems.* New York, NY: McGraw Hill

Grisham, T. (2009). The Delphi technique: A method for testing complex and multifaceted topics. *International Journal of Managing Projects in Business, 2*(1), 112–130.

Gritsch, M. (2009). Electronic copies vs. hard copies: An unhappy medium? Allied Academies International Conference. *Academy of Information and Management Sciences. Proceedings, 13*(2), 27–31.

Hall, E. B. (2009a). Strategic planning in times of extreme uncertainty. In C. A. Lentz (Ed.), *The refractive thinker: Vol. I. An anthology of higher learning* (pp. 41–58). Las Vegas, NV: The Lentz Leadership Institute.

Hall, E. B. (2009b). The Delphi primer: Doing real-world or academic research using a mixed-method approach. In C. A. Lentz (Ed.), *The refractive thinker: Vol. II. An anthology of higher learning* (pp. 3–27). Las Vegas, NV: The Lentz Leadership Institute.

Hall, E. B., & Hinkelman, R. M. (2007). *Perpetual innovation: A patent primer.* Morrisville, NC: LuLu Press.

Helmer, O. (1967, November). *Systematic use of expert opinions.* (DDC No. AD662320) (Report #P-4732). Santa Monica, CA: The RAND Corporation.

Job Service North Dakota. (2006). *UIICE: Unemployment insurance Internet claims entry.* Bismarck, ND: Author. Retrieved from www.jobsnd.com

Kahan, A. (1999). Learning from Mont Fleur: Scenarios as a tool for discovering common ground. *Deeper News 7(1).* Global Business Network (GBN). Available electronically at www.gbn.org

Katz, R. (2003). *The human side of managing technological innovation* (2nd ed.). New York, NY: Oxford University Press.

Keisler, J. M. (2002). Attribute-based differentiation of alternatives. *Journal of Multicriteria Decision Analysis, 11*(6), 315–326.

Kreger, L. (1999). Paper & the information age. *Information Management Journal, 33*(4), 38–42.

Lee, S., & Kim, M. (2010). Inter-technology networks to support innovation strategy: An analysis of Korea's new growth engines. *Innovation: Management, Policy, & Practice, 12(1),* 88–104.

Martino, J. P. (1972, August). Technological forecasting is alive and well in industry. *The Futurist.* Bethesda, MD: The World Future Society.

Millett, S. M., & Zelman, S. T. (2005). Scenario analysis and a logic model of public education in Ohio. *Strategy & Leadership, 33*(2), 33–40.

Naisbitt, J. (1982). *Megatrends: Ten new directions transforming our lives.* New York, NY: Warner Books.

Naisbitt, J. (2006). *Mind set: Reset your thinking and see the future.* New York, NY: HarperCollins.

Naisbitt, J., & Aburdene, P. (1990). *Megatrends 2000: Ten new directions for the 1990's.* New York, NY: Avon Books.

Narayanan, V. K., & Zane, L. J. (2009). Inventing a future for strategic leadership: Phenomenal variety and epistemic opportunities. *Journal of Strategy and Management, 2*(4), 380–404.

National Telecommunications and Information Administration (NTIA) of the U.S. Department of Commerce (DOC). (2009). Digital nation: 21st century America's progress toward universal broadband Internet access. Washington, D.C.: U.S. Government. Available at http://www.ntia.doc.gov/reports/2010/NTIA_internet_use_report_Feb2010.pdf

Par, B. (2010, July). Mashable readers choose real books over e-books. *Mashable.* http://mashable.com/2010/07/24/e-book-real-book-results/

Perrottet, C. M. (1996, January). Scenarios for the future. *Management Review,* 43–46.

Pierce County Library System. (n.d. a). *Reserve a computer: Book online reservations in advance.* Tacoma, WA: Author. Retrieved from http://www.pierce countylibrary.org

Pierce County Library System. (n.d. b). *Tools for tough economic times.* Tacoma, WA: Author. Retrieved from http://www.piercecountylibrary.org

Sackman, H. (1974, April). *Delphi assessment: Expert opinion, forecasting, and group process.* A report prepared for United States Air Force Project (Report #R-1283-PR). Santa Monica, CA: The RAND Corporation.

Sandler, M., Armstrong, K., & Nardini, B. (2007, Fall). Market formation for e-books: Diffusion, confusion or delusion? *JEP: the journal of electronic publishing 10(3).* doi: 10.3998/3336451.0010.310.

Schumpeter, J. A. (1942/2008). *Capitalism, socialism and democracy.* New York: Harper Perennial Modern Classics.

Stabo, T. (2009). Fishing report: Stream model to project future fishing in waterways. Washington, D.C.: U.S. Geological Survey.

Sterry, L. F., & Hendricks, R. W. (1997). *Exploring technology.* Menomonie, WI: T&E Publications.

Sweeney, C., & Lynch, P. (2010). Adaptive post-processing of short-term wind forecasts for energy applications. Wind Energy, n/a. doi:10.1002/we.420

Tapscott, D., & Williams, A. (2006). *Wikinomics: How mass collaboration changes everything.* New York, NY: Penguin Group, Inc.

Tharp, P. (2009). As more people file for unemployment online, libraries seek computer-literate volunteers. Richmond, IN: Palladium

Toffler, A. (1971). *Future shock.* New York, NY: Bantam Books.

U.S. Department of Energy (DOE). (2010, July 28). *Key events timeline.* Deepwater Horizon BP Spill. Available electronically at http://www.energy.gov/open/oilspilldata.htm

U.S. Nuclear Regulatory Commission (NRC). (2009, April 30). *Fact sheet: Chernobyl-backgrounder.* Available electronically at http://www.nrc.gov

Willmore, J. (1998, September). Scenario planning. *Info-line Issue 9809.* Alexandria, VA: American Society for Training and Development.

About the Author

 Dr. Lois D. Wiley Anderson holds a Bachelor of Science (BS) in Secondary Education and a Master of Science in Human Resource Development (MSHRD) from Indiana State University, an MBA from Indiana Wesleyan University; and a Ph.D. in Technology Management from Indiana State University. She holds a Certificate of Mediation from Indiana State University. Dr. Lois is currently a faculty member of Capella University in the School of Business and Technology. She consults in support of online higher education, and in the areas of training and development programs for business and industry. She serves as the Sr. Technology Consultant for SilkWeb Consulting & Development (www.silkwebconsulting.com).

Dr. Lois is a member of Epsilon Pi Tau and Phi Kappa Phi. At Indiana Wesleyan University, she was recognized as Outstanding Professional. She was a Chester G. Taylor Scholarship recipient. Her professional experiences include Corporate Training Manager for a Manufacturing Subsidiary of Tomkins, PLC. She taught as an adjunct business instructor at several colleges and universities. She served as a Doctoral Academic Operations Chair and mentored numerous doctoral learners to completed doctoral degrees.

Presentations and published works include: Research contributor to the third edition of *"Training Manager Competencies: The Standards," the International Board of Standards for Training, Performance, and Instruction (IBSTPI); Giving Away A Piece of My Soul: Connecting with the Online Learner; Learner Loyalty: Initiating Long-Term Allegiance in an Online Doctoral Program through Successful Student Orientation and Preparation, and Renewable Energy Technology Textbook* to be released in 2011.

To reach Dr. Lois for information on any of these topics, please e-mail: DrLois@silkwebconsulting.com

CHAPTER 3

The Next Big Disruptive Innovation: Can You Imagine a World Without Intel?

Dr. Edgar Jordan

Virtually everything that has electrical power applied in some way depends on the electrical properties of materials such as silicon dioxide and, to a lesser extent, germanium dioxide. Even the control circuits of household irons depend on devices known as field programmable gate arrays made from these materials. The same is true for almost everything in common usage today that is powered by electricity. A more obvious example would be the cell phone and the communications networks that allow for modern methods of staying in touch. What might happen if these ubiquitous materials reached the end of its usefulness and was replaced by some entirely different material? What might happen to Intel, Advanced Micro Devices (more commonly known as AMD), or Motorola if the new material results in electronic devices becoming drastically smaller? What organizational changes might be necessary for a large, multinational company to adapt to a new technology that fundamental to the industry of which the company is a part but is radically different from that which is in current use? What leadership styles would be best suited to makes such organizational adaptation most efficient, or is organizational change required at all? Finally, what materials are likely to emerge into the market place as the replacement for silicon dioxide and when might that emergence occur? These are the questions the Jordan study (2010) sought to address.

The advancements in semiconducting material used in all electronic circuits could be reaching the physical limits. The semiconductor manufacturing industry leaders recognize the eventuality of such an event (International Technology Roadmap for Semiconductors [ITRS], 2005, 2006, 2007). Industry leaders consider the event will occur at some distant future. As shown in Figure 1, the individuals who have contributed to the publications of the International Technology Roadmap for Semiconductors anticipate evolving technologies will follow a downward sloping linear trajectory based on Moore's law for some time to come (Brock, 2006).

The physical limit of silicon dioxide, the material forming the basis for the bulk of electronic circuits, is at the 10 nanometer (nm) scale (Kish, 2004; Olukotun & Hammond, 2005). Considerable research is available on technologies at scales far below the 10 nm limit (Bernstein, Frank, Gattiker, Haensch, & Nassif, 2006; Hiramoto, Saitoh, & Tsutsui, 2006; Kuekes, Snider, & Williams, 2005; Lane & Kalil, 2005; Rieffel & Polak, 2000). When new materials are mature enough to be used in marketable products, the shift from silicon dioxide to the new materials might cause a technological discontinuity and prove disruptive to current leaders in the industry (Anthony & Christensen, 2005; Christensen, 1997; Christensen, Anthony, & Roth, 2004; Christensen & Raynor, 2003; Forster, 2006).

The Jordan study (2010) involved a modified Delphi method to engage members of the semiconductor industry in projections concerning the potential transition to new materials. The basic Delphi methodology was modified to include individuals who were experts by virtue of their position, their expertise in their respective organizations and the breadth of their knowledge of the industry as a whole. Based on their success in attaining their position in the respective organizations, the individuals selected acted as proxy for other forms of expertise. The Rand Corporation 1944 developed the Delphi method at the conclusion of World War II in an effort to facilitate projections by groups of experts while avoiding the hazards of group think (Hall, 2009; Dalkey, 1969). The method developed into an iterative methodology consisting of posing questions to a selected group of experts, analyzing the responses, and reframing the next round of questions in the context of the answers as a way to build on consensus (Hall, 2009).

In research using the Delphi method of information gathering, experts are not initially aware of the other members' responses. This helps individual panel members develop their answers to posed questions without the influence of the group. The approach has been used successfully to develop long range strategic plans for the federal government (Keeney, Hasson, & McKenna, 2006), and is often used in the medical community as a method for developing standards of care as well as identifying more efficient management approaches (Dinnebeil, McInerney, & Hale, 2006; Lummus, Vokurka, & Duclos, 2005; MPhil, Lovell, & Harris, 2006; Schnyer et al., 2005; Vazques-Ramos, Leahy, & Hernandez, 2007). The focus of recent research using the Delphi method has been issues of leadership in the normative sense (Baker, 2005; Huth, 2006; Lentz, 2007; Limas, 2005; Sheridan, 2005; Stiles, 2005). In recent work, the Delphi method was used to address the question of organizational structure (Champion, 2007; Rumble, 2006; Uhlman, 2006).

PROBLEM DISCUSSION

The information in Figure 1 suggests the leaders of the semiconductor industry expect technology development to follow a path that combines system-on-chip technologies (the vertical axis in the figure) with increasingly sophisticated kinds of systems-in-package (the horizontal axis in the figure) to achieve smaller scale devices. The units depicted on the vertical axis become ambiguous at scales smaller than 22 nm. The depiction points to the 10 nm theoretical limit based on the underlying physics of such devices (Eisenhardt, 1988). Whatever the transition point there should be a movement to a new technology at some time in the future, as depicted by the cloud labeled beyond Cosmos; the very area of uncertainty in the technological future that Jordan (2010) sought to clarify. Cosmos is an acronym for complimentary symmetry metal oxide semiconductor. The semiconductor industry leaders acknowledge the need for such transition will occur.

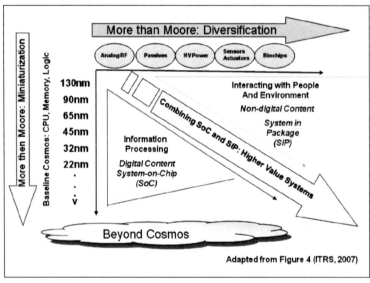

Figure 1. Vision of Future Developments as Expressed in ITRS Material.

The technologies enabling digital electronics come from the electrical properties of silicon and germanium when impurities are introduced to enhance the semiconducting properties of these elements (Lecuyer, 2006; Lojeck, 2007; Morris, 1990; WebElements, 2007). The discovery of the electrical properties of silicon and germanium led to the invention of the discrete transistor in 1948 and the development of the planar transistor in the 1960s (Morris, 1990; Orton, 2004). The advent of the planar transistor generated a coalescence of developments facilitating the emergence of the business environment of the 21st century (Brock, 2006; Forster, 2006; Hirooka, 2006; Intel, 2006; ITRS, 2005, 2006; Kish, 2004; Lecuyer, 2006; Lojeck, 2007; Morris, 1990; Rezvani, Baytas, & Leveen, 2006).

Shortly after the demonstration of the commercial viability of the integrated circuit based on the planar transistor, Gordon Moore articulated what has become known as Moore's law. According to Moore's law, the number of devices on a chip will double approximately every 2 years (Brock, 2006; Intel, 2006; Morris, 1990; Olukotun & Hammond, 2005; Schaller, 2005). While Moore's law was primarily an observation about economics, the law has become the driving force behind much innovation resulting in the powerful electronic systems that are essential to the global economy. The original intent of Moore's law was to describe the effect of market forces on what was then the emerging semiconductor manufacturing industry, but the effect of Moore's law has been to prescribe organizational activity (Grossi, Royakkers, & Dignum, 2007).

The continued pursuit of Moore's law as an industry goal might be approaching the end of its utility for several practical reasons (Brock, 2006). One reason concerns power consumption and the resultant heat generation. In the 1980s, processors drew approximately a 10th of a Watt of power. The Pentium IV™ draws approximately 100 Watts of power (Kish, 2004; Olukotun & Hammond, 2005). If the Pentium processor is used as a model, the next generation of processors will require exotic cooling methods that would be impractical for use by the general consumer.

Goal of the Jordan Study

The goal of Jordan's qualitative descriptive research study (2010) was to explore the leadership issues, strategic planning issues, and organizational structures considered by market leaders in the semiconductor manufacturing industry in response to emerging technologies. The modified Delphi approach was appropriate because individuals working in the field acted as surrogates for the experts who were typically members of a Delphi panel. These individuals were acceptable experts because of many years of experience in the field, because of their academic background, and due to their current position.

Emerging technologies such as nanocomputing and quantum computing technologies could lead to disruptive innovation. Leadership styles and organizational structures optimized to react to technological discontinuities and potentially disruptive technologies are defined as the styles and structures best suited to allow a market leader to capitalize on the introduction of a "skills destroying technological discontinuity" (Tushman & Anderson, 1986, p. 439).

The Study Methodology and Research Questions

The Jordan study (2010) sought to answer the following questions: (a) the appropriate strategic planning time frame for emerging technologies, (b) the organizational structures considered important to investigate, and (c) the leadership styles that should be used to implement the required organizational changes. Based on the areas of inquiry, the questions posed to the Delphi panel were as follows:

1. Considering that new materials being researched could result in technological discontinuity possibly leading to disruptive innovation, what strategic planning time-frame is envisioned for the emergence of replacement materials for semiconductors?

2. What emerging technologies seem most promising?

3. Considering that new materials being researched could result in technological discontinuity possibly leading to disruptive innovation, what changes would be required in organizational structures to incorporate the new technologies into product lines?

4. What leadership approaches are envisioned as being required to integrate emerging technologies into product offerings?

The panel was also asked what the emergent technology will likely be.

Panel Recruitment

Two separate efforts were made to recruit panel members for this study because a weaker than expected response was obtained from the first attempt. Unfortunately, the subsequent recruitment didn't yield a large response either. Although Delphi studies are commonly done with small group sizes of 12 experts or smaller, a larger panel size would have allowed Jordan to be much more confident in the quantitative results generated. The basic demographic data reported by the panel members were gathered in Round One. One panel member chose not to respond to the demographic portion of the data gathering. Other questions existed to which individual panel members did not respond.

The panel was gender biased, skewing to male. The mean age of the panel was 46 years old. The perspective of the panel members was dominated by industry, but the panel members were approximately evenly divided between observer and participant. The mean number of years in their position at the time of the study was 5 years. Most of the panel members reported being relatively recently moved to their current position.

Interestingly, the members of the panel overwhelmingly reported that they had studied organizational change. This implies the panel would have been familiar with subjects such as leadership methods and organizational forms. The organizational structure the panel members reported was generally hierarchical in nature, and panel members were evenly divided about whether to expect change in the future.

The purpose of the Round Two surveys was to further clarify responses the panel members gave to the research questions in Round One and explore important issues tangential to the questions directly pertaining to the research. The questions were in open-ended form to further elicit the thoughts of the panel members and further refine concepts not directly addressed in the research. Likert-based questions, mean values for the panel, other groups, and combined data sets were computed.

As part of the Round One questions, the panel was asked the open ended question of when a replacement might emerge. The responses to this open-ended formed the basis for the ordinal form of the emergence question asked in Round Two. There was surprising consistency between the respondents from the two panels. Jordan was impressed with the credentials of the panel was it had been formed. He said "The range of perspective and insight of the panel as a whole is quite remarkable. The research is strengthened by that range" (2010, p. 119).

JORDAN'S FINDINGS

The results of the big question as to when disruptive technologies might emerge are shown in Table 1. The panel members and other respondents were of the opinion that a new technology would emerge between 2020 and 2035 at the 50% confidence level as can be seen in Table 1. The panel members and other respondents were of the opinion that a new technology would emerge between 2030 and 2035 at the 90% confidence level as can be seen in Table 1. The

Years until Disruption

Round One Panel Response (using original interval data)

Years until disruption (n=10); using original responses, not categorized

	Low	High	Year (+2010 yrs)	
Range	5	100	2015	2110
Mean	22.5		2032.50	
Median	12.5		2022.50	
Mode	15.0		2025.00	
STDV	29.15		29.15	

Round One Panel Response (Grouped into frequency/percentage table)

	<2020	<2030	<2040	<2050	<2060	<2070	<2080	<2090	<2100	<2110
Decades until Disruption	5/50%	3/30%	1/10%	0	0	0	0	0	0	1/10%

Round Two Panel Response (using frequency per decade)

Years until disruption (n=10); using original responses, not categorized

50% Confidence Level

	<2020	<2030	<2040	<2050	<2060
Round Two Panel Response (n=8)	4/50%	3/38%	1/13%		
Round Two Other Groups (n=4)	3/75%	1/25%			
Round Two Other Groups (n=12)	7/58%	4/33%	1/8%		

	Low	High	Year (mid-point)		Year (max)	
Range	1	3	2015	2035	2020	2040
Mean	1.5		2020		2025	
Median	1.0		2015		2020	
Mode	1.0		2015		2020	
STDV	0.67		6.74		6.74	

90% Confidence Level

	<2020	<2030	<2040	<2050	<2060
Round Two Panel Response (n=8)	1/13%	3/38%	2/25%	1/13%	1/13%
Round Two Other Groups (n=4)	1/25%	2/50%	1/25%		
Round Two Other Groups (n=12)	2/17%	5/42%	3/25%	1/8%	1/8%

	Low	High	Year (mid-point)		Year (max)	
Range	1	5	2015	2055	2020	2060
Mean	2.5		2030		2035	
Median	2.0		2025		2030	
Mode	2.0		2025		2030	
STDV	1.17		11.68		11.68	

Table 1. *Years until Disruption*

details of the panels' responses at this level are contained in Table 1. Members of the panel suggest that other time frames might be more illuminating, but they did not provide specific year changes. The members of the panel and the other groups received instruction to provide insight into the meaning of the term *product emergence*. In general, responses pertained to the commercial viability of the technology. One respondent suggested having production-ready devices available for viability testing would constitute emergence.

In Round One, the panel was asked an open-ended question

about what new technologies might supplant the current semiconducting materials. In Round Two, four choices for replacement technologies emerged from the Round One open-ended question that were presented in the context of a Likert-like scale of importance. The question following offered the opportunity for further open-ended discussion concerning the possible replacement technologies. When asked to choose a technology likely to emerge, the panel members felt a dielectric similar to silicon dioxide would be very important and a nanotube based technology, or something more exotic, would be important. When asked what other technologies might prove important, the panel members suggested carbon based (i.e. graphene), quantum computing, and spin transfer-based technologies. Such technologies have a scale of a single device that is multiple orders of magnitude smaller than the theoretic limit for materials in use in electronic circuits today.

The panel members had no opinion about the importance of flat or hierarchical organizational structures in the event of organizational change. The panel members found an organization based on a meritocracy was important. The members of the other groups had no opinion about the importance of a flat organization and felt both hierarchical and meritocratic forms were important.

When the Round Two data sets comprised of the eight panel members and four individuals providing additional information from the LinkedIn™ groups were combined, the responses were neutral pertaining to flat or hierarchical forms, but meritocracy was important. When asked what other organizational structure might be important, one of the panel members suggested the question was irrelevant. The same panel member suggested the important factor in organizational performance was existential threat. Any organizational structure would outperform others given that condition.

The leadership approach is central to organizational change. When asked what approach to leadership would best facilitate the introduction of potentially disruptive innovation, the panel members felt situational, transformational, and collaborative approaches were important. The panel members had no opinion about servant leadership forms. The members of the other groups felt transformational and collaborative forms of leadership were important but had no opinion about situational or servant forms of leadership. When the data sets were combined, the outcomes were consistent with the panel members' opinion.

The survey included a question about what other important organizational issues should be addressed. The panel members felt addressing structures facilitating entry-level empowerment with clear upper mobility paths and improving asynchronous communications was important. The panel members felt aligning all levels of the organization to overall goals were very important. They had no opinion about developing an effective bridge between corporate leadership and local presence for an international corporation.

The panel members expressed no opinion about the development of a framework for international business ethics. The members of the other groups felt all five categories of organizational challenges were important. The results of the combined data sets suggest organizational alignment is very important (i.e., 5 on the survey scale), and the other four categories are important (i.e., 4 on the survey scale).

The panel members' responses provided insight into how professionals and observers in the semiconductor industry expect emerging technologies to affect the industry. The panel members considered (a) when a replacement technology might emerge, (b) what the emergent technology might be, (c) what organizational structures would best facilitate such an emergence, and (d) what leadership approaches would prove to be important to affect the emergence. The panel members considered other organizational issues that would be important in the context of potentially disruptive innovation.

CONCLUSION

The semiconductor industry has pursued Moore's law as if this law were an organizational imperative. However, industry leaders have acknowledged that the current semiconductor technologies have a physical limit that will be reached at some indeterminate point in the future. Both government and industry are investing heavily in technologies that could produce individual devices on the molecular scale or smaller. Some of these more exotic materials might be mature enough to emerge into the market place within a few decades. In fact, if the respondents to this study are correct, emergent technologies will be fully developed as early as 15 years and almost certainly within 30 years.

The Jordan study (2010) revealed several things of significance concerning organizational and leadership studies as well as providing insight into the panel members' thinking about emergent technologies for the semiconducting material current in use. The study also provided insight into the use of social networking sites, such as LinkedIn™ for conducting social research.

In particular, the panel was very clear that an organizational structure that is based on merit is of primary importance. The panel was equally clear that the leadership styles best suited to lead an organization in times of technological change were a blend of transformational and collaborative. Equally as important is that the panel was not enthusiastic about situational or servant leadership forms.

According to the experts in the study, new and breakthrough technology is coming far faster than maybe most prior studies suggest. The silicone-based technology that has dominated the electronics and computer industry for more than half a century appears poised for a major disruptive change. Likely within the next 5 to 25 years, a technology will emerge—but not necessarily be fully developed—to replace the silicone chip.

The panel was of the opinion that the material that may emerge to replace the current semiconductors would likely bring a considerable shift in the dimensions of individual devices. The technologies and the likelihood of emergence were:

- A biologic (e.g. protein) based material—80%

- Nanotubube (or similar carbon based material) or some material more exotic—60%

- Material generally the same as currently in use—40%

What this list says as much as anything else is that a replacement material generally the same as what we use now is the least likely. The panel was equally direct about when an emergent material may be ready for commercial use. These drastic shifts may not be all that far off in time. The 2010 Nobel Prize for Physics was awarded for the development of a form of carbon that has width and length that can be measured in inches while only having the thickness of a single atom. This material has many of the properties of the semiconducting material currently in common use.

The fundamental question addressed in the Jordan study was whether the emergence of new materials would prove disruptive. The literature on disruptive innovation suggests the impact can be devastating on organizations that are not in a position to make the necessary adjustments to adapt appropriately to emerging technologies. Given the research being conducted into exotic semiconductor materials, the potential for disruptive innovation to occur when the materials become commercially available cannot be ignored. Aggressive well-grounded transformational leadership will likely be required for such corporations to adapt to the future they are discovering.

References

Anthony, S. D., & Christensen, C. M. (2005, February). Can you disrupt and sustain at the same time? *Harvard Management Update,* 3–4.

Baker, K. J. (2005). A model for leading online K—12 learning environments. D.M. dissertation, University of Phoenix, United States—Arizona, i-171. Retrieved May 5, 2008, from Dissertations & Theses @ University of Phoenix database.

Bernstein, K., Frank, D. J., Gattiker, A. E., Haensch, W., Ji, B. L., & Nassif, E. J. (2006, July/September). High-performance CMOS variability in the 65-nm regime and beyond. *IBM Journal of Research & Development, 50*(4/5), 433–449.

Brock, D. C. (Ed.). (2006). *Understanding Moore's Law: Four decades of innovation.* Philadelphia, PA: Chemical Heritage Foundation.

Christensen, C. M. (1997). *The innovator's dilemma: When new technologies cause great firms to fail.* Boston, MA: Harvard Business School Press.

Christensen, C. M., & Raynor, M. E. (2003). *The innovator's solutions: Creating and sustaining successful growth.* Boston, MA: Harvard Business School Press.

Christensen, C. M., Anthony, S. D., & Roth, E. A. (2004). *Seeing what's next: Using the theories of innovation to predict industry change.* Boston, MA: Harvard Business School Press.

Dalkey, N. C. (1969, June). The Delphi method: An experimental study of group opinion. (Report #RM-5888-PR). Santa Monica, CA: The RAND Corporation.

Dinnebeil, L., McInerney, W., & Hale, L. (2006). Understanding the roles and responsibilities of itinerant ECSE teaches through Delphi research. *Topics in Early Childhood Special Education, 26*(3), 153–166.

Eisenhardt, K. M. (1988). Agency and institutional theory explanations: The case of retail sales compensation. *Academy of Management Journal, 31*(3), 488–511.

Forster, N. (2006). The impact of emerging technologies on business, industry, commerce and humanity during the 21st century. *The Journal of Business Perspective, 10*(4), 1–27.

Grossi, D., Royakkers, L., & Dignum, F. (2007). Organizational structure and responsibility: an analysis in a dynamic logic of organized collective agency. *Artif Intell Law, 15*(3), 223–249.

Hall, E. (2009). Strategic planning in times of extreme uncertainty. In C. A. Lentz (Ed.), *The Refractive Thinker: Vol 1. An Anthology of Higher Learning* (pp. 41-58). Las Vegas, NV: The Lentz Leadership Institute.

Hiramoto, T., Saitoh, M., & Tsutsui, G. (2006, July/September). Emerging nanoscale silicon devices taking advantage of nanostructure physics. *IBM Journal of Research & Development, 50*(4/5), 411–418.

Intel. (2006). *Intel silicon processes technology: One generation ahead—to keep you in the lead.* Retrieved from http://222.intel.com/technology/silicon

International Technology Roadmap for Semiconductors. (2005). *2005 edition: Emerging research devices.* Retrieved http://from www.itrs.net/reports.html

International Technology Roadmap for Semiconductors. (2006). *2006 update: Overview and working group summaries.* Retrieved from http://www.itrs.net/reports.html

International Technology Roadmap for Semiconductors. (2007). *2007 edition: Executive summary.* Retrieved from http://www.itrs.net/Links/2007 ITRS/Home2007.htm

Jordan, E. A. (2010). The semiconductor industry and emerging technologies: A study using a modified Delphi Method. (Doctoral dissertation). University of Phoenix, Phoenix, AZ.

Kish, L. B. (2004, April). Moore's Law and the energy requirement of computing versus performance. IEE Proceedings—*Circuits, Devices & Systems, 151*(2), 190–194.

Kuekes, P. J., Snider, G. S., & Williams, R. S. (2005, November). Crossbar nanocomputers: Crisscrossing assemblies of defect-prone nanowires. *Scientific American,* 72–80.

Lane, N., & Kalil, T. (2005, Summer). The national nanotechnology initiative: Present at the creation. *Issues in Science and Technology, 21*(4), 49–54.

Lecuyer, C. (2006). *Making silicon valley: Innovation and growth of high tech, 1930–1970.* Cambridge, MA: The MIT Press.

Lentz, C. (2007). *Strategic decision-making in organizational performance: A quantitative study of employee inclusiveness* (Doctoral dissertation). Available from ProQuest Dissertations and Theses database. (UMI No. 3277192).

Limas, J. R. (2005). *The influence of performance appraisal systems on leadership development. D.M. dissertation, University of Phoenix, United States—Arizona, i–261*. Retrieved from Dissertations & Theses @ University of Phoenix database.

Linked In. (2010, May 14). [Description]. Retrieved from http://www.linkedin.com.

Lojeck, B. (2007). *History of semiconductor engineering*. Berlin, Germany: Springer.

Lummus, R. R., Vokurka, R. J., & Duclos, L. K. (2005, July). Delphi study on supply chain flexibility. *International Journal of Production Research, 43*(13), 2687–2708.

Morris, P. R. (1990). *A history of the semiconductor industry*. London, UK: Peter Peregrinus, Ltd.

Olukotun, K.., & Hammond, L. (2005, September). The future of microprocessors. *Association of Computing Machinery, 3*(7), 26–34.

Orton, J. (2004). *The story of semiconductors*. New York, NY: Oxford University Press.

Rezvani, F., Baytas, A., & Leveen, S. (2006, September). The U.S., Japan in the global semiconductor industry. *The Journal of American Academy of Business, 10*(1), 44–109.

Rieffel, E., & Polak, W. (2000, September). An introduction to quantum computing for non-physicists. *Association of Computing Machinery Computing Surveys, 32*(3), 300–335.

Schaller, R. R. (2005). Technological innovation in the semiconductor industry: A case study of the International Technology Roadmap for Semiconductors (ITRS). Dissertation Abstracts International, 65 (02), 837, 605A. (UMI No. 3122570)

Schnyer, R. N., Conboy, L. A., Jacobson, E., McKnight, P., Goddard, T., . . . Moscatelli, F. (2005). Development of a Chinese medicine assessment measure: An interdisciplinary approach using the Delphi method. *The Journal of Alternative and Complementary Medicine, 11*(6), 1005–1013.

Sheridan, E. (2005). Intercultural leadership competencies for United States business leaders in the new millennium. Dissertation Abstracts International, 66(04), 1425A. (UMI No. 3172360)

Stiles, H. J. (2005). The charter school leader: An investigation of leadership qualities, knowledge, and experience. Dissertation Abstracts International, 66(04), 1238A. (UMI No. 3172361)

Tushman, M. L., & Anderson, P. (1986, September). Technological discontinuities and organizational environments. *Administrative Science Quarterly,* 31(3), 439–465.

Vazques-Ramos, R., Leahy, M., & Hernandez, N. E. (2007). The Delphi method in rehabilitation counseling research. *Rehabilitation Counseling Bulletin, 50*(2), 111–118.

WebElements. (2007). WebElements periodic table [Periodic Table]. Available from WebElements Period Table, http://www.webelements.com/

About the Author

Dr. Edgar A. Jordan is a retired Navy Commander who has several accredited degrees including a Doctor of Business Administration (DBA) from University of Phoenix, School of Advanced Studies. He has a Master of Science (MS) in Engineering Acoustics as well as a Bachelor of Science (BS) in Electrical Engineering from the Naval Postgraduate School. Additionally, he has a Bachelor of Science (BS) in physics from Weber State University.

Dr. Ed is the President of 5 Rings Solutions, LLC; a small, but enthusiastic, engineering consulting firm under contract to the U.S. Navy to provide expert advice concerning advanced sonar design. From a technical perspective, he is primarily focused on advanced transduction technologies as well as signal processing techniques. Dr. Ed provides expert advice to the government on long range strategic planning focused on the introduction of emerging technologies into combat systems. He also provides assistance concerning budget development, program articulation, and management in these specialty areas.

Dr. Ed was elected to membership of Sigma Xi, The Scientific Research Society, and is an active member of the Academy of Management.

To reach Dr. Ed Jordan for further information, please e-mail: eajordan@msn.com

CHAPTER 4

Leadership Strategies for Embedding Innovation in Organizational Culture

Dr. Olivia Herriford

The characteristics of any organization, including effectiveness and the manner in which it performs, are embedded in its culture (Kotter & Heskett, 1992; Schein, 1992). If leaders desire to have an innovative organization culture, innovation has to go beyond being espoused to being embedded in practices and assumptions about and how things get done throughout the organization. To perform well under conditions of rapid external and internal expansion and transformation, innovation and change must become essential elements of organizational culture (Nacinovic, Galectic, & Cavlek, 2010).

Leaders create and sustain organizational culture, making them accountable for building a culture of innovation. Managers at all levels of an organization must transparently exercise interest and commitment to the activities that foster innovation and nurture the development of a culture that sustains it (Zairi & Al-Mashari, 2005). The strategic challenge facing most organizations is to continually generate good ideas and convert them into products or services that are successful in their markets. To innovate continually, organizations must shift their innovative thinking out of the laboratory, real or symbolic, and encourage it throughout the enterprise. A culture of innovation must be nurtured by leadership until it permeates everything the organization does, everywhere, all the time (Tilina & Ispas, 2009).

Innovation Defined

Drucker (2002) defined *innovation* as the effort to create purposeful, focused change in an enterprise's economic or social potential. That effort is a guided evolutionary process based on experimentation, judgment and selection of what works and does not work (Pohlmann, Gerbhardt, & Etzkowitz, 2005). Although business innovations, particularly those in technology, are most associated with the term, innovation occurs in all types of organizations and communities (Jaskyte, 2004).

Organizational leaders consider innovation as a core competency essential to achieving strength in the markets in which they compete. Innovation can be a system and its principles can be taught (Denning, 2004). Like all competencies and capabilities, innovation is about education; information, demonstration, discourse, practice and discipline.

There is a distinction between innovation and invention, the latter being another way in which innovation is viewed. Denning (2004) reminded us that there is no guarantee that an idea or invention will become an innovation. "The practice of innovation is not a practice of inventing. Innovation requires attention to other people, what they value and will adopt; invention requires only attention to technology" (Denning, 2004, p. 15).

A closer relationship between innovation and outcome was well-defined by Drucker (1985) in *Innovation and Entrepreneurship*. Most successful innovations result from a conscious search for opportunities in seven areas which are described in Table 1.

TABLE 1. OPPORTUNITIES FOR INNOVATION
(Drucker, 1985, 2002)

Opportunity	Description
Unexpected events	Unexpected successes of failures; outside events
Incongruities	A gap between reality and common belief aspects that do not fit together
Process need	A bottle neck in a critical process
Change of industry structure	New business models, distribution channels, modes of business
Demographics	Changes in groups by age, politics, religion, income, etc.
Change in perception	Change in the way people see the world
New knowledge	Application of new knowledge, often involving scientific advances or the convergence of multiple strands of knowledge

Innovation's focus is on opportunities created by breakdowns, problems, changes, and challenges. Drucker (2002) made a point of caution that although new knowledge (e.g. technology, inventions) gets most of the attention as a source of innovation, it is only one of the opportunities and the most challenging of them all. Innovation from new knowledge takes time, has a high casualty rate, and the outcomes are the most unpredictable.

An example of the challenge and its fatal attraction is the fate of many business startups that assume innovation is the creation of new products and services. Startup entrepreneurs struggle to bring their products and service to the market because they often fail to consider and integrate the other opportunities as potential starting points (Pohlmann et al., 2005).

Characteristics of a Culture of Innovation

Organizational culture is created by the beliefs and assumptions about what and how things are done within an organization. Culture manifests as the perceived values of the organization and its leadership through the rituals (celebrations, communications, policies, etc.) that support those beliefs, assumptions and values (Kotter & Heskett, 1992; Schein, 1992). An organization's culture frames shared motives, common behaviors, joint attitudes, and patterns of meaning that guide the actions of an organization's or community's members. Until one focuses and reflects on these attributes, a culture's impact is usually subconscious.

Understanding organizational culture is important because there is a clear relationship between organizational culture and performance (Kotter & Heskett, 1992). Cultures that focused on all stakeholders and levels of leadership, outperformed firms that did not have string cultural traits.

Strong cultures are characterized by the following attributes (Herriford, 2002; Kotter & Heskett, 1992).

- Most employees, at all levels, share a set of relatively consistent values and methods of doing business

- New employees adopt these values quickly

- Outsiders perceive the organization as having a certain "style"

- Employees have a high level of engagement and motivation in employees

- Executives maintain a commitment to developing and communicating the vision and purpose of the organization

- The organization is transformational with a strong base of transactional practices

- There are few, if any, subcultures have conflicting values and practices with the overall culture

Examples of US organizations with strong cultures are Apple, Southwest Airlines, Starbucks, Walmart, Toyota, Boys & Girls Club of America, and Medtronic (Denison & Mishra, 1995; Hrywna & Rogers, 2010; O'Reilly, 1989; Stanley, 2007).

In a world of accelerating change, corporate culture will be an even more important factor in determining success or failure in firms. Adaptability is the key to effectiveness. An adaptive organizational culture is one that emphasizes commitment to its key constituencies and values innovative ideas and process-creating change, what Avolio & Bass (1993) call a *transformational culture.*

Recalling that innovation can mean either new ideas or new practices, Denning (2004) asserted that since ideas have no use until they are put into practice, innovation means the adoption of a new practice in a community. From this perspective, innovation is a social transformation in a community, further suggesting its linkage to culture.

A culture of innovation is an environment where everyone in the organization is busy finding ways to help themselves and customers continuously improve performance without special urgings from leadership (Denning, 2004). Culture defines the assumptions about how and why things are done based on leadership influence rather than direction. An organizational culture of this nature can be a primary source of competitive advantage and can pay off steadily over the years if innovation can become a way of life.

An organization's culture defines the elements and parts that have an impact on innovation processes, therefore to sustain innovation, the structure and development of innovation systems must be embedded in the cultural foundation of an organization (Pohlmann et al., 2005). Cultural values and norms are powerful means of stimulating creativity and innovation. When a value system of innovation permeates the entire organization, people behave accordingly (Nacinovic et al., 2010).

Managing innovation implies rules of cooperation and social behavior. Underlying a culture of innovation is a mechanism of interchange or foundation of social rules. Consequently, an organization's innovation must be viewed as social systems, which support their strategy. Looking at innovation systems as a social system might bring back simplicity to innovation studies and openings for new fields to explore in innovation strategies (Pohlmann et al., 2005). Given this social aspect of innovation, the linkage to culture is stronger. To create a culture of innovation, there are behaviors and systems that must be everywhere and embraced by everyone within the organization (Stopper, 2006).

Leadership Role in the Development of Organizational Culture

Strong organizational cultures are associated with strong and competent leadership (Bass & Avolio, 1993). Organizational cultures can be made more innovative and performance-enhancing with time and leadership that goes beyond traditional measures of effective management (Kotter & Heskett, 1992). The difference is emotionally intelligent leaders with a passion for people and results (Goleman, 2000), build leadership capability throughout the organization's culture and systems (O'Connor & Quinn, 2004). Complex situations and challenges call for both leadership and innovation to be a shared responsibility throughout the organization. As a result, effective leadership is increasingly becoming an organization's capacity to influence collective work. The more versatile an organization is in its abilities to build upon its leadership capacity, the more effective the collective work. The emerging approach to both organizational leadership and innovation is based upon the creation of shared meaning and a system strategy that leverages communication, relationships, fairness, trust, power, truth, flexibility, and empowerment.

Strong, high-performing cultures must be adaptive with internal capabilities to turn challenges into opportunities (Bass & Avolio, 1993; Kotter, 1996; Kotter & Heskett, 1992), which is the essence of innovation. Innovation is about leading change, which presents a dichotomy. Innovation is much easier to embrace than change. For this reason, leadership behaviors and practices that embed the processes and disciplines of innovation also embed adaptability to change. Leadership, process and social systems become the DNA essential for sustaining performance and innovation (Price, 2006). Sustained innovation must start with how people lead and are led (Nacinovic et al., 2010).

Leadership Strategies for Embedding Innovation in Organizational Culture

Leaders contribute to project success at all levels by providing clarity of vision, formulating and communicating strategy, developing goals and outcomes, and giving teams the flexibility to deal with the issues themselves (Zairi & Al-Mashari, 2005). Leaders must also be innovators, seizing opportunities for improvement.

Effective communication of organizational vision, values, and goals helps to achieve a three-way alignment of strategy, culture, and performance. When people know what they do is meaningful and critical to the success of the organization, engagement and a sense of urgency are created that minimizes questioning and resistance (Kotter, 1996; Zairi & Al-Mashari, 2005). For example, by providing clarity of the desired outcome and letting a team decide on *how* to deliver that outcome, senior managers can have the biggest impact on innovation because clarity encourages idea formulation, new concepts, and feasibility (Zairi & Al-Mashari, 2005).

Managing innovation requires belief systems which are modeled throughout the organization. "It is a fact that no single manager can control all elements of an innovation system" (Pohlmann et al., 2005, p. 6). Most agree that leaders create, maintain, and/or change culture and new entrants to the environment are the most impacted. The individuals in the middle of the organizations with longer tenure, however, experience culture from multiple perspectives because they often the link between the upper and lower levels of an organization and its culture (Herriford, 2002; Huy, 2001).

In mature organizations, managing innovation usually involves two roles, a passionate project leader (or champion) and a senior sponsor. These two roles may not be sufficient. In a study of companies with sustained innovation accomplishment (Vincent, 2005), there was an informal network of people, usually middle managers, who served as translators between the language, subculture and needs of the sponsor's world and that of the champion's world. When brought together, these two worlds can clash, creating disruption, distraction, and conflict. Recognizing the gap between the two subcultures of the sponsor and the champion, leaders take the first step in getting beyond the language and cultural barriers to the results they desire from their investment in innovation. Vincent's (2005) study of successful innovation management in established organizations identified mid-level to senior executives 'behind the scenes' balancing the needs of innovation with the needs of operational control. They did not consider themselves sponsors and instead described themselves as *ambassador, catalyst, interpreter, filter, third party,* and *in-between guy.* Vincent (2005) drew upon the metaphor of midwife and labeled them as *innovation midwives* that "nurture, develop and integrate innovations that may otherwise be rejected by the organization's core" (p. 41).

Innovation midwives are sensitive to the core business strategy yet able to counteract the inertia that can stifle new ideas for how and where the organization can be revitalized. Similar to the focus of a traditional midwife, an innovation midwife is concerned with the health of the mother, the core business, and the child, the viability of the innovation. Innovation midwives take on the challenge of bridging the subcultures of the sponsor and the innovator by justifying innovation, finding relevance to the core business, reducing risk, and resolving conflicts (Vincent, 2005).

Events that highlight innovation, such as innovation fairs or innovation days, bring attention to projects progress, quality, challenges, practices, and success. Such events not only offer shared learning experience, but most important to sustainability, they also become rituals of the culture (Zairi & Al-Mashari, 2005).

Drucker (1985) identified five elements of the process of innovation (see Table 2). Leaders at all levels of an organization play an essential role in establishing a culture of innovation and change by means of the behaviors, practices, and policies they adopt and implement (Price, 2006). Sustaining a culture of innovation is a long-term strategy of embedding key elements into the way things get done in an organization. Those elements include systems, tools and techniques, measurement and metrics, team-building, empowerment, clear understanding of requirements, customer focus, and technological competence (Zairi & Al-Mashari, 2005). Just as important, leaders need to design and implement processes that build on personal motivation and ability to innovate throughout the organization.

The practices in Table 2 are primarily social. They further demonstrate that the work of innovation, although it requires discipline, is about an awareness of people and what they need. The same principles apply to leaders who must model the innovation they wish to realize. In his research of the behaviors of innovators, Denning

TABLE 2. ELEMENTS OF THE PROCESS OF INNOVATION (Drucker, 1985)

Process Element	Description
Searching for opportunity	Noticing opportunity in one of the seven innovation sources (see Table 1)
Analysis	Applying a consistent decision-making process: Developing a project of business plan, identifying costs, resources, and people, analyzing risk and benefits
Listening	Going out into the community, listening for concerns, finding what they are receptive to, adapting the proposal to match
Focus	Developing a single articulation of the central idea and sticking to it despite temptations to embellish or extend prematurely
Leadership	Positioning the practice or technology to be the best of breed

(2004) identified the common patterns of their behaviors, which further characterize a culture of innovation.

Building the personal skills essential to modeling the practices above requires its own discipline. Organizational leaders must commit themselves to creating an environment conducive to innovation, raising their tolerance for risk, experimentation, and the occasional failure. Most leaders will need a coach or teacher to assist with the assessment and effective use of emotional intelligence competencies; self-awareness, self-management, social awareness and relationship management (Goleman, 1998); all of which are foundational to the personal practices of innovation above. Similarly, employees have to be empowered and trusted to seek opportunities on their own initiative, but they do need guidance, training, and

TABLE 3. PERSONAL FOUNDATIONAL PRACTICES OF INNOVATION (DENNING, 2004)

Practice	Description
Awareness	Ability to perceive opportunities and concerns, distinguishing them from personal agenda and concerns; ability to overcome cognitive blindness.
Focus and Persistence	Ability to maintain attention on the mission and avoid distractions; holding to the mission amidst chaos, challenge, or opposition; refusal to give up in the face of obstacles and challenges to the mission.
Listening and Blending	Listening for deeply held concerns and interests and adapting actions to fit (finding the win-win)
Declarations	Ability to make simple, powerful, moving, eloquent declarations that create possibilities and open attractive new world for others
Offers	Making and fulfilling offers that bring services, practices, or artifacts of value to customers; organizing groups and managing their commitments toward delivery of the results; maintaining a deep commitment to doing whatever is needed to obtain the results
Networks and Institutions	Gathering allies, defending against objectors, and creating institutions to further the innovations, develop common standards, and widen its acceptance
Learning	Making time to learn new skills, acquire new knowledge; making well-grounded assessments in preparation for new learning and action

the tools to implement whatever solutions they come up with (Tilina & Ispas, 2009).

Development of an organizational culture that supports and fosters innovation must be supported by innovation-oriented human resources practices (Nacinovic et al., 2010). Organizations need to invest in training emphasizing the necessary skills, processes, and practices. Performance-based reward systems that recognize employee contributions and outcomes must be established. Team development for leadership and team-based activities that support collective work is also essential.

Conclusion

The capability of an organization to continuously innovate and transform itself is a function of culture—embedded everywhere and in everyone. This capability becomes ingrained in the organization's social and structural fabrics as deeply as it becomes evident in the beliefs and values of the people.

Leaders influence organizational culture and innovation through a strategy of personal, social, and structural motivation and capabilities (Grenny, Maxfield, & Shimberg, 2008). People are motivated when innovation is linked to organizational mission and values and there is regular investment in the development of their skills. Social motivation is created by ensuring that every manager from the front line to the C-suite teaches, models, and coaches the behaviors that support innovation. Leaders develop social capabilities using four strategies. They provide people the assistance requires for new practices; identify obstacles and establish support networks to overcome them; create a safe environment for ideas to be expressed; and provide people with the authority, information, and resources necessary to turn ideas into innovation. Structural motivation comes from formal reward systems and informal events that create consistency, provide incentives, and recognize innovation as a ritual of the culture. Structural capabilities are the tools, facilities, information, proximity to others, feedback mechanisms, policies, and work processes that support all of these strategies.

A culture of innovation enables an organization to continuously seize upon opportunities to improve, not only products and services, but how things are done, which is the culture itself. So an innovative organization is not only turning ideas into innovation, the organization is also continuously building upon the strengths of its culture. Senge (1994) stated, "learning organizations have been invented, but they have not been innovated" (p. 6). A culture of innovation innovates itself, creating the reinforcing feedback process of a true learning organization.

References

Bass, B. M., & Avolio, B. J. (1993). Transformational leadership and organizational culture. *PAQ, 112–121.*

Denison, D. R., & Mishra, A. K. (1995). Toward a theory of organizational culture and effectiveness. *Organization Science, 6*(2), 21.

Denning, P. J. (2004). The social life of innovation. *Communications of the ACM, 47*(4), 5.

Drucker, P. F. (1985). *Innovation and entrepreneurship.* New York, NY: HarperCollins.

Drucker, P. F. (2002). The disciple of innovation. *Harvard Business Review, 80*(8), 10.

Goleman, D. (1998). *Working with emotional intelligence.* New York, NY: Bantam Books.

Goleman, D. (2000). Leadership that gets results. *Harvard Business Review, 78*(2), 78–90.

Grenny, J., Maxfield, D., & Shimberg, A. (2008). How to have influence. *MIT Sloan Management Review, 50*(1), 6.

Herriford, O. (2002). *High-technology organizational culture and emotional intelligence.* Unpublished doctoral dissertation, University of Phoenix, Phoenix.

Hrywna, M., & Rogers, K. (2010). 50 best nonprofits to work for in 2010. *The Nonprofit Times.*

Huy, Q. N. (2001). In praise of middle managers. *Harvard Business Review, 79*(8), 72–79.

Jaskyte, K. (2004). Transformational leadership, organizational culture, and innovativeness in nonprofit organizations. *Nonprofit Management & Leadership, 15*(2), 16.

Kotter, J. P. (1996). *Leading change.* Boston, MA: Harvard Business School Press.

Kotter, J. P., & Heskett, J. L. (1992). *Corporate culture and performance.* New York, NY: Macmillan.

Nacinovic, I., Galectic, L., & Cavlek, N. (2010). Corporate culture and innovation: Implications for reward systems. *International Journal of Social Sciences, 5*(1), 6.

O'Connor, P. M. G., & Quinn, L. (2004). *Organizational capacity for leadership.* San Francisco, CA: Jossey-Bass.

O'Reilly, C. (1989). Corporations, culture, and commitment: Motivation and social control in organizations. *California Management Review,* 17.

Pohlmann, M., Gerbhardt, C., & Etzkowitz, H. (2005). The development of innovation systems and the art of innovation management - Strategy, control and the culture of innovation. *Technology Analysis & Strategic Management, 17*(1), 7.

Price, R. (2006). Change: Innovation in the corporate DNA. *The Journal for Quality and Participation,* 5.

Schein, E. H. (1992). *Organizational culture and leadership.* San Francisco, CA: Jossey-Bass.

Stanley, T. L. (2007). Generate a positive corporate culture. *Supervision, 68*(9), 3.

Stopper, B. (2006). Innovation at Whirlpool: Embedment and sustainability. *Human Resource Planning, 29*(3), 3.

Tilina, D., & Ispas, C. (2009). The challenge of innovation in the economic crisis. *Annals of Danube Adria Association for Automation & Manufacturing (DAAAM) International, 20*(1), 1.

Vincent, L. (2005). Innovation midwives: Sustaining innovation streams in established companies. *Research and Technology Management,* 9.

Zairi, M., & Al-Mashari, M. (2005). Developing a sustainable culture of innovation management: A prescriptive approach. *Knowledge and Process Management, 12*(3), 13.

About the Author

Dr. Olivia Herriford, a change consultant and business and leadership coach, holds a Bachelor of Science (BS) in Applied Mathematics from Northrop University, a Master of Business Administration (MBA) from the University of Phoenix, John Sperling School of Business and a Doctor of Management (DM) from the University of Phoenix, School of Advanced Studies. She is adjunct faculty for John F. Kennedy University and University of Phoenix teaching and developing curriculum for business and leadership courses in the undergraduate business and MBA programs.

Olivia is a certified Gazelles International™ business coach with expertise in assisting social sector organizations and high-growth businesses with development and execution of growth strategies. She applies her certification as a mediator to work as a volunteer in the Center for Human Development's conflict resolution programs and to practical approaches to conflict management workshops and coaching.

Olivia is a board member of East Bay Coaches, a chapter of the International Coaches Federation (ICF), the Bayview Hunters Point YMCA, and the Attitudinal Healing Connection of Oakland. In addition to ICF, she is a member of the American Society for Training and Development, the International Society for Performance Improvement, the American Society of Association Executives, and the International Association of Facilitators.

Leveraging the research and findings from her dissertation, Emotional Intelligence and High-technology Organizational Culture, Doctor Olivia has developed and delivered workshops on Creating a Culture of Leadership, Cultural Sensitivity and Conflict Management, and Influencing Sustainable Change. Her first book, Everyday Mediation, in collaboration with conflict coach, Marilynn Hall, will be published this winter.

Dr. Herriford lives in Walnut Creek, California and travels to Kenya on a regular basis, where she works with social sector organizations and businesses through the Kenya Institute of Management in support of Kenya's Vision 2030.

CHAPTER 5

The Three Ps of Leadership: Pulling, Pushing, and Patting

Dr. Sheila Embry

Technological innovations and innovative leadership are popular terms for twenty-first century managers. During the 2000 decade, inventions such as iPod®, iPhone®, iPad®, broadband, data compression, digital audio players, text-messaging, smartphones, flash drives, YouTube®, open source, free software, blogs, wikis, file-sharing, Skype, Facebook, Twitter, Bluetooth, microblogging, peer-to-peer technology, and smartboards became common in the workplace (America, 2010). The internet search engine Google reached such high popularity in the last decade that it became defined as a verb, i.e., *Google it* (Selanikio, 2008). Additionally, innovative leadership is also about "processes, business models, and leadership" (Strickland, 2010, para. 2).

Leadership has evolved throughout the centuries from Great Man theory through transformational and transactional theories. While some theories overlapped through the decades, there are indications to support the theory that we have moved from the Great Man theory of leadership that was popular in Nineteenth Century (Chemers, 2009). Though some political figures still claim that they are anointed to their position by a higher power, the majority of modern leaders do not make such claims. Charismatic and trait theories, made popular in the 1920s and 1930s, still have their place in modern leadership theory. No one trait is exclusively associated with effective leadership theory; however, social scientists during the 1920s and 1930s did identify intelligence, charisma, and physical stature as indicators of perceived leadership traits (Chemers, 2009).

Twentieth century leadership included the 1940s and 1950's movement away from social sciences toward the psychological / behavioral area of group theory including Maslow's hierarchy of needs and McGregor's Theory X and Theory Y. These theories provided a paradigm shift away from organizational successes tied to the leaders toward organizational successes tied to the employees. The next evolution was contingency leadership theory that began in the 1960s. Contingency theory included path-goal, situational, and principle-centered theories based on the idea that leaders' characteristics must be relevant to the followers and group goals for success (Rost, 1993).

Twenty-first century leadership includes transactional and transformational theories. Transactional theory was based on a political exchange barter system and was created in the late 1970s. Because of the *give to get* relationship, most transactional relationships were short-lived. Transformational leadership, made popular in the 1980s and 1990s, was based on leaders and collaborators working together on mutual purposes (Rost, 1993). Transformational strategies were reciprocal, relied on trust, empowered employees, and encouraged ownership of organizational goals (Colbert, Kristoff-Brown, & Bradley, 2008). As the 2000 decade came to a close, a sub-group of the transformational theory was evolving: individual and collective efficacy. This expansion of transformational theory lists credibility, task-relevant competencies, trustworthiness, justice, and fairness in its traits (Chemers, 2009).

The majority of Nineteenth and Twentieth Century leadership theories were patriarchal. Patriarchal management was created on an intentional linear, horizontal path toward goal outcomes (Field, 2010). Patriarchal leadership was commonly defined as one person, beyond question, making final decisions authoritatively; a singular, ultimate leader (Kanyoro, 2006). Twenty first century leadership is a blend of patriarchal and evolving matriarchal that includes singular (patriarchal) and shared (matriarchal) leadership (Kanyoro, 2006). Matriarchal leadership is created on a spiral not a linear path. Choosing a spiral path adds intuition, receptivity, relatedness, and wholeness to linear goal outcomes to create cycles of fulfillment to goal completion (Field, 2010).

The current theory presented, the 3Ps of Leadership (3Ps), is a matriarchal theory. The 3Ps is a deceptively simplistic model that assists leaders to transition out of patriarchal, 20th Century authoritative leadership toward matriarchal, 21st Century shared leadership. As technological innovations requires employees to work smarter, quicker, and from more locations, the 3Ps will assist leaders to ensure their 21st Century employees are fully engaged; employee morale is high; and that employees, managers, and leaders have the potential toward professional and organizational fulfillment and actualization. Adding the 3Ps of Leadership's pushing, pulling, and patting, and Schuttler's (2008) Laws of Communication's red, yellow, and green to Tuckman's well-established 1965 Group Development Model of forming, storming, norming, performing and adjourning creates a new, synergetic triangulation of theories to assist managers to turn nebulous everyday commands into succinct, sustainable team successes.

Background

Understanding team development is an important asset for leaders, managers, and supervisors. In 1965, Tuckman created a group development model that included the stages of forming, storming, norming, and performing. In 1977, Tuckman and Jenkins added the adjourning stage, also known as the mourning stage (Abdui, 2010). For teams that do not adjourn, a fifth stage was added, transforming or re-norming, depending on the level of performance (Rickards & Moger, 2000). Tuckman's model became a worldwide standard for group development. In 1998, the National Council of Boy Scouts of America adapted Tuckman's theory and created the Wood Badge for the Twenty-First Century around it (Stolowitz, 1998).

The introduction stage, forming, identified individuals desiring to be accepted into the team. Members remained individuals but avoided conflict and controversial issues in their desire to be accepted. The second stage was storming. In this stage, differences in ideas and issues arose. Tolerance, patience, and conflict resolution skills were needed to successfully maneuver through to stage three. Norming, stage three, identified team members releasing individual ideas and issues and joining together into one team to accomplish group goals. The fourth stage, performing, found the teams working without conflict and without need for external supervision. Team members were interdependent, motivated, knowledgeable, and decision-makers (Tuckman, 1965). The fifth and final stage was adjourning or transforming. At the final stage, teams would break up because the task or project was over or would have the potential to move from performance teams to transformational teams wherein they could produce major changes through synergic transformational management (Abudi, 2010).

Clear communication is a requisite answer for leading teams. In 2008, Schuttler created the Laws of Communication model. Using a two-dimensional grid, the theoretical framework suggested supervisor leadership and communication predicted employee behavior (see Figure 1). With a traffic light metaphor, Schuttler categorized organizations into red, yellow, and green zones. The model's framework allowed managers to identify critical concerns (red), as well as elements needing to be watched (yellow), and other elements working well (green) (Schuttler, 2008).

Critiquing the traditional communication model of message, sender, receiver, and feedback, Schuttler suggested a dynamic, relationship-driven approach was more effective. Schuttler's (2008) analyses indicated that trust, morale, visibility, attentiveness, education, and change, significantly influenced performance. By listening to and encouraging employee input, supervisors empowered employees to succeed individually and accomplish goals organizationally. Effective communication skills positively influenced employee performance and job satisfaction and were essential for the survival and growth of organizations (Schuttler, 2010).

Through the Laws of Communication model, Schuttler (2008) identified specific, measurable supervisor communication behaviors used in development and training and incorporated the behaviors into the model. Schuttler indicated red zone leaders tended to be myopic, micromanaging employees. Yellow leaders tended to fight fires rather than function proactively while green leaders walked the talk with role modeling and mentoring. Following the assessment of the efficacy of leader communication (i.e., red, yellow, or green), organizational leaders used Schuttler's (2008) two-dimensional grid to predict employee performance. With knowledge about the relationships between variables relevant to communication skills and employee performance, leaders are in a stronger position to make changes positively influencing employee morale, turnover, and productivity.

Embry's 2009 Study

In 2009, Rouse and Schuttler developed the Supervisor Leadership and Communication Inventory (SLCI) to assess organizational performance based on supervisor leadership communication and employee performance. Based on the Laws of Communication model, each member of the organization rates supervisory leadership, supervisory communication, and employee performance (Schuttler, 2010). Using the SLCI, Embry (2009) conducted a mixed-methods study to examine the relationship between leadership, communication, and employee performance within one federal agency directorate. The goal was to test the correlation between the predictor variables of perceived supervisor leadership and communication and the criterion variable of employee performance within a large federal agency.

Using a two-dimensional grid to show how supervisor leadership and leader communication could predict employee behavior, the survey contained 53 questions to measure supervisor leadership, leader communication, and employee performance; three demographic questions; and three open-ended questions to allow the participants to offer comments, suggestions, and recommendations for better leadership communication and better employee performance. One research question asked, what relationship, if any, exists between supervisors' leadership and employees' performance. Quantitative responses indicated that supervisors' leadership was significantly correlated with employee performance. High levels of supervisor leadership were associated with high employee performance, and low supervisor leadership was significantly associated with low employee performance.

The purpose of the mixed-methods study was to discover relationships between supervisor leadership, supervisor communication, and employee performance. Qualitative responses indicated effective leadership, management visibility, and attentiveness were the top themes to improve employee performance and supervisor leadership (Embry, 2009).

Tuckman modeled that teams were formed, stormed, normed, and adjourned or performed (with optional transformed) (Abudi,

Figure 1. Schuttler's Two-dimensional Grid
of Organizational Communication.

Note: Copyright 2008 Richard Schuttler. Reprinted with permission of the author.

2010). Schuttler modeled that the traditional communication model of message, sender, receiver, and feedback belonged with the 20th Century patriarchal leadership theories. His two-dimensional grid illustrating how leader communication styles affected employees' performances moved the traditional communication model into the 21st Century with its matriarchal leadership attributes of trust, morale, transparency, quality, mission fulfillment, and adaptation to change (2010).

Pulling

To bridge the gap from Tuckman's 1965 model to Schuttler's 2008 model, the 3Ps of Leadership model is needed. When a 3P Leader begins with a new team, he or she will communicate theories and ideas thoroughly and may choose the traditional patriarchal exercise of directing the team. In addition, the 3P Leader will also metaphorically pull the team toward the leader's strategy of producing, of ensuring quality assurance, and of determining successful results through consistency and communication including conflict resolution, assertiveness, team charters, the Laws of Communication model, and other beyond the box communication strategies.

During this first stage of the model, the 3P Leader will be the one with the responsibility; will talk more than team members; will write more reports than team members; and will facilitate more presentations, meetings, forums, etc. than the team members. While the 3P Leader is pulling the weight of the team, he or she is also assessing strengths and capabilities of the new team. Comparing this stage to the Schuttler Laws of Communication model, Stage One—pulling is the red, or lower left grid (Schuttler, 2008). Comparing this to Tuckman's Group Development model, Stage One—pulling occurs in stages one and two—forming and storming (Tuckman, 1965). A 3P Leader's communication style during this stage is informative, structured directive guidance that is task based.

Pushing

Continuing the metaphor of pulling the team on a rope, once a leader can feel the slack on the line (which is translated that he or she is no longer having to pull the team members along but that they are beginning to align with the 3P Leader's ideas), the leader should move from stage one—pulling to stage two—pushing. In stage two—pushing, the 3P Leader, having observed that the team is capable of taking on more responsibilities, moves from in front of the team to in back of the team. The team members take on more leadership by talking more, writing more, facilitating presentations, meetings, forums more, and taking responsibility more. The 3P

Leader stands behind the team, observing them, coaching them, and pushing them from the back whenever the team or a specific team member stalls.

Stage two—pushing compares to stage three—norming in Tuckman's Group Development model. It also compares to the yellow or middle grid of Schuttler's Laws of Communication model (Schuttler, 2008; Tuckman, 1965). A 3P Leader's communication during this stage is coaching, single-loop, and objectives based.

Patting

As the team continues to work together and move from the norming to the performing stage, the 3P Leader moves from stage two—pushing to stage three—patting. The 3P Leader moves from pushing behind to walking along side the team members. Regularly, the 3P Leader will reach out and pat a specific team member. The pat may be to move a team member back in line with the forward movement of the team as a whole, or the pat may be an affirmative feedback pat to reinforce good behavior. In the patting stage, team members are clear in their roles and responsibilities but reach out for clarification of taskings and priorities as needed.

Stage three—patting compares to stage four—performing in Tuckman's Group Development model and to the green, or upper right, grid of Schuttler's Law of Communication model (Schuttler, 2008; Tuckman, 1965). In this stage, the team steps up and not only follows the guidance of the 3P Leader, but begins to offer ideas, suggestions, and guidance for the betterment of the team. A 3P Leader's communication during this stage is open, interactive, and proactive. Team communication moves up to comprehensive mission and vision based dialogues. 3P Leaders offer mentoring, role modeling, and succession planning. When new team members enter the group, this 3P Leader cycle begins again.

TABLE 1. COMPARISON OF THREE THEORIES: EMBRY, SCHUTTLER, TUCKMAN

Leadership's 3Ps	Communication Law	Group Development
Patting	Green	Performing & Transforming
Pushing	Yellow	Norming
Pulling	Red	Forming & Storming

Though simplistic, the pulling, pushing, and patting stages cannot be taken out of order. At the inauguration of the team or at its restructuring, team members look to the 3P Leader for action, for modeling, for discipline, and for guidance to ensure their actions are in alignment with what is required to ensure a successful team experience. If the 3P Leader continues to stand in front of the team pulling once team members are comfortable with their roles and responsibilities instead of standing behind the team pushing and coaching, the manager will appear to be micromanaging. This type of management performance will encourage poor team performances.

If the 3P Leader continues to stand behind the team and push when the team has moved to the patting stage and is capable of making decisions and producing on their own, the 3P Leader will appear to be self-interested not group-interested. This type of leadership will encourage mediocre performance in the team. Walking along side the team and course correcting by mentoring and role modeling will encourage self-directed, valued, and responsible team members.

To get back to the business of leading while staying current with valid innovative technologies, this author recommends three theories: Tuckman's Group Development model (1965), Schuttler's Laws of Communication model (2008), and Embry's 3Ps of Leadership model. A collaborative use of each of these theories will assist to turn every day, undefined challenges into targeted, managerial guidance to encourage collaborative, team successes.

During phases one and two of team development, forming and storming, a 3P Leader should use stage one, pulling, to move the team from the red to the yellow zone in communication. In these stages, team members are still acting as individuals and are not working together toward team goals yet. They could blame others, including management, for poor delivery times or poor quality (Schuttler, 2010). Leaders should provide directed guidance, structured oversight, and regular check-ins to move the team into the norming phase and yellow stage.

When the team moves to norming phase and the yellow zone, leaders should use stage two, pushing, to provide encouragement and coaching to propel their teams forward toward their goals. Employees will start to work together as a team and to offer ideas for improvement; although often these ideas will be remakes of trendy, out of the box ideas (Schuttler, 2010). To move the team from the norming, yellow zone to the performing / transforming green zone, a 3P Leader must work to ensure they are not in a fighting-fires mode during this time but are offering consistent coaching guidance.

When the team moves to the performing / transforming green zone, the 3P Leader should use stage three, patting, to mentor employees. Communication is high and open between leaders and teams as the group works together to refine processes and skills. There is trust between team members and leadership (Schuttler, 2010). A 3P Leader should include team members in decision-making and treat them as equal stakeholders. Team members should provide timely, succinct feedback, and they should model the behavior they want to encourage in their team.

Moving teams through the group development phases of forming, storming, norming, performing, transforming and through the red, yellow, green stages of the Law of Communication by using the

3Ps of Leadership will provide employees with feelings of empowerment, of being valued, and of being responsible for their own successes. Identifying with the organization's sense of purpose, team members will have a positive impact on others in the organization and elsewhere (Schuttler, 2010). Leaders moving from pulling through pushing to patting will begin pulling the team's responsibilities. However, with the development of the team through the pushing stage to the patting stage, the responsibilities shift from the manager to the team (see Figure 2).

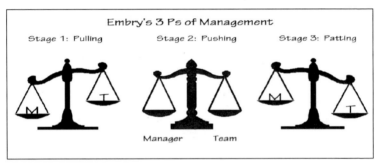

Figure 2: Responsibility Distribution Within Three Stages of the 3Ps of Leadership

Conclusion

Teams operating at a high level of performance distribute responsibilities throughout each of the team members. Communication is open among the members and management. The team is optimistic. Optimistic team members who communicate openly inside and outside the team create trusting work environments. Leaders who know when to pull, when to push, and when to step aside and pat as needed will have greater successes at developing and leading winning teams in the twenty-first century environment where new technologies and ever evolving innovative ways of performing tasks will continually challenge leaders and team members.

References

Abudi, G. (2010). *The five stages of project-team development: Improve team performance.* Retrieved from www.pmhut.com/the-five-stages-of-project-team-development

America's best history: US Timeline—2000s. (2009). Retrieved from http://americasbesthistory.com/abhtimeline2000.html

Chemers, M. (2009). *Leadership, change, and organizational effectiveness.* Santa Cruz, CA: University of California. Retrieved from http://www.almaden.ibm.com/coevolution

Colbert, A., Kristoff-Brown, A., & Bradley, B. (2008). CEO transformational leadership: The role of goal importance congruence in top management teams. *Academy of Management Journal, 51*(1), 81–96.

Embry, S. (2009). A mixed methods study: Understanding employee performance at The Department of Homeland Security. *Sheila 2009: From ABD to Success.* Scott Valley, CA: CreateSpace Publishers.

Field, J. (2010). *The spiral: A universal symbol of transformation coaching sanctuary.* Retrieved from www.coachingsanctuary.com

Kanyoro, M. (2006). *Challenges to women's leadership.* Retrieved from http://www.wordywca.org

Rickards, T., & Moger, S., (2000) Creative leadership processes in project team development: An alternative to Tuckman's stage model. *British Journal of Management, 4,* 273–283

Rost, J. (1993). *Leadership for the Twenty-first Century.* New York, NY: Praeger Publishers.

Schuttler, R. (2008). *Laws of communication.* Retrieved from http://lawsofcomm.com/default.asp

Schuttler, R. (2010). *Laws of communication: The intersection where leadership meets employee performance.* Hoboken, NJ: John Wiley & Sons.

Selanikio, J. (2008–01–18).The invisible computer revolution. *BBC News.* Retrieved from http://news.bbc.co.uk

Stolowitz, M. (1998). *Wood Badge for the Twenty-First Century.* Retrieved from www.woodbadge.org/BoyScout

Strickland, L. (2010) Risk Innovation or Be Beaten by Those Who Do. *The Street*. Retrieved from http://www.thestreet.com/story/10866232/

Tuckman, B. (1965). Development sequence in small groups. *Psychological Bulletin 63*(6) 384–399.

About the Author

Dr. Sheila Embry holds a Doctor of Management (DM) in Organizational Leadership from University of Phoenix School of Advanced Studies, a Master of Arts (MA) in Human Resources Development from Webster University, and a Baccalaureate (BA) in Business Administration from McKendree College. She is also a graduate of Spencerian College and a multiple graduate of the Federal Law Enforcement Training Center.

Dr. Sheila is a Unit Chief with a large federal agency where prior assignments included *Branch Chief, Program Manager, Supervisor,* and *Officer.* Previously she served as *Local Projects Coordinator* for Congressman Romano L. Mazzoli, and worked with the Hilton Hotels Corporation, and with The Irvine Company.

Additional published works include her dissertation: *A Mixed Method Study: Understanding Employee Performance at the Department of Homeland Security; Leadership and Communication; Key Essentials To Employee Performance, Morale, Turnover, and Productivity; From ABD to Success; A Life on (Temporary) Hold: From ABD to DM in 366 days + 3 years; Communication: The Key to Performance;* and *Have We Tipped Yet: Are We Ready To Demand Ethical Behavior From Our Leaders?*

A member of the University of Riverside Advisory Council, International Women's Writing Guild, NaNoWriMo, and Refractive Thinkers®, she writes a weekly blog entitled *Doctor's Orders* (http://sheila embry.wordpress.com/). Look for her next book, *Dear Cousin: Written Memories from Inspirational Everyday Events* in the Fall of 2010.

To reach Dr. Sheila Embry for information on any of these topics, please e-mail: drembry@ymail.com

CHAPTER 6

Innovation and Gender Equality Through the Lens of Competition

Dr. Jane Dennehy

Beyond Winning and Losing

Work is increasingly becoming externally and internally competitive as organizations reshape and respond to changing and often unpredictable landscapes in local, national and global markets. Exploring why some people avoid competition, by choice or exclusion, while others seek it out, is important to understanding why some talented and skilled individuals may be denied the opportunity to contribute and implement ideas.

For most of us, the context of competition is grounded in sport which is where we find scarcity and challenge models operating. The scarcity model prepares for only one winner (zero-sum) for example the Football World Cup. The challenge model however offers the opportunity for any number of participants to win as found in a running race where dead heats are possible (Miner & Longino, 1987). However transplanting successful sporting models of competition into the world of management can be limiting and result in the constriction of individual and organizational innovation.

References to games and rules at work are usually clouded in ill-defined notions that lack transparency where referees are absent. Such games can also become entangled with individual perceptions, attitudes, and behaviours (Edwards &Wajcman, 2005; Schein, 2007). Proposing that competition is a multi-dimensional and fluid dynamic, interacting on our relationships at work, suggests a value in defining and examining some of those dimensions.

Work: Nothing Lasts Forever

Western societies are increasingly experiencing multiple versions of households when only a few decades ago the single breadwinner was the basis for many career models, economic activity, and the foundation of the nuclear family (Crompton, 1999). Alongside this major shift in approaches to work, is the increasing participation rate of women in the labour market across all sectors and occupational positions (Bradley, 1996). Experiencing a traditional linear career is no longer the only option available, as witnessed by the growth of portfolio careers which can be a concoction of contracting, business start-ups and consultancy (Reich, 2000; Rifkin, 2004).

The impact of such change is apparent in how the career model one may want and seek to attain may not be available in the medium and long-term. This in turn places responsibility on the individual to continually innovate their skills and knowledge to ensure their market value remains relevant. Beck (1992, 2002) suggests in his individualization thesis that the labour market has three key dimensions; education, mobility, and competition, which are all, interrelated as we navigate a world of systems, and which continue to divest responsibility to us as individuals. The term individualization should not to be confused with individualism which describes the structural transformation of social institutions highlighting one's agency as the dominant feature in the relationship between the individual and society.

For women however, the work environment has additional complications with high rates of women in part-time work, prevailing gender pay gaps, occupational and hierarchical segregation, and the double burden women predominantly carry in terms of care and career (McRae,2003; Brannen, 2005; Schein, 2007; Connelly, 2008). How such issues are measured and reported continue to use wide-scale applications such as the 2010 UK Chartered Institute's report, which states that equal pay will not be achieved till 2067. While the importance of such metrics ensures that gender equality in the labour market remains visible, the supporting rhetoric is arguably somewhat stagnant, repetitive, and simply un-motivating. Unable to reflect the complexities of organizations or the individuals who populate them, the time for new thinking and innovation becomes increasingly urgent.

What Rules? What Game?

In Dennehy's (2010) study, competition was explored to understand how this dynamic was experienced and perceived by managers, and what impact this had on their career. Aligning the scenarios of games and rules and ultimately competition in the management arena is, Dennehy (2010) argues, limiting to those that may participate, as well as those who do not, whether by choice or exclusion. Furthermore, the examination explored how and in what ways competition and competitive relationships in management are gendered.

Gender: Not Just About Women

The role of gender in Dennehy's (2010) study places importance on arguing that to understand how gender interacts with competition and management requires defining the concept. Butler (2004) states that gender is "not exactly what one *is* nor is it precisely what one *has*" (p 42). This is developed by the work of Le Feuvre (1999) who argues that gender is not so much about biological differences but more about social processes and how relationships taking place in society can incorporate and encourage hierarchies favouring one individual over another. Gender as Dennehy (2010) states is a social construction, which can produce, maintain, and use a range of discourses, operating in isolation or in combination across different relationships, locations, and cultures.

Applying gender to management, Wajcman (1999) and McDowell (1997) discuss the ways in which men and women's behaviour and attitudes can be influenced by social and professional stereotypes assigned to their gender. For example, some women seek to control what they perceive as their gender weakness by embracing the attributes of their male colleagues. Such women are often cited as the group who act, dress, and speak like men to lessen the visibility of their gender. Similarly, some men adhere to perceptions of acceptable behaviour such as leaving their caring roles and relationships at the front door of the office rather than to share the stresses, which affect their performance and well-being.

While gender has been caught up in the metrics of equality, competition has largely remained invisible and in-articulated among managers. Rethinking how and why managers are important in all organizations and how they manage competition and competitive relationships at work can, as Dennehy (2010) argues, be a catalyst for looking at how gender and competition can be better defined and understood.

Competition: A Multi-Dimensional Dynamic

For some managers, competition is only ever considered as negative. For other, competitions are merely a necessary part of operating in a market economy. For a few, competition offers a motivating and meaningful contribution to their working lives and leisure activities. To begin the process of identifying the multiple facets of competition, Bradley's (1999) model of gendered power was reinterpreted to develop a competition model using eight dimensions. This is shown below (see Figure 1).

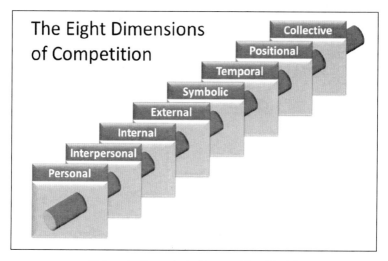

Figure 1: Dennehy's Competition Model

At the centre of a manager's experiences are the relationships they have with the organization which includes superiors, peers, and subordinates (Margretta, 2002). How cultures at work determine meanings and definitions of competition for example, is important to understanding the parameters within which managers define their experiences and perceptions of what they do and how they do it. How relationships change within organizations may be the result of a promotion, departmental restructuring, career breaks, or the employment of new peers or superiors. Identifying and analyzing the range of relationships a manager may have over the course of their career and the role of competition in how they develop different relationships was used by Dennehy (2010) to examine the interplay with gender.

Exploring different relationships at work is a strand, which runs through Dennehy's (2010) project examining the influence of hierarchies to gain insights into how competition manifests in the lives of managers at work. On each rung of the ladder, competitive issues will be present in terms of external and internal demands. Investigating how such pressures impact on the processes and outcomes of management is important to defining and understanding competition as a multi-functioning dynamic (Dennehy, 2010).

The Research Process

The criteria used in Dennehy's (2010) study for a manager was responsibility for staff and/or budget. The final sample was 32 interviews with a gender ratio split of 3/1 women to men. The interviews were carried out in the United Kingdom and Australia. Dennehy (2010) uses grounded theory as the methodological approach and after completing all 32 interviews she considered that some points of theoretical saturation were reached, providing useful insights and meeting the research objectives. The number of participants takes into account that qualitative research usually has smaller numbers than quantitative research projects and that the data collected using qualitative methods will produce intense and rich information (Oakley, 2000; O'Connell Davison et al., 1994). Dennehy (2010) stated that while she did not aim to produce generalizations due to the size of the final sample, her aim was to offer descriptions of human behaviour that influence a sector of the labour market—management.

Time as a Fixed Resource

Temporal competition has its roots in the working culture where the underpinning premise is—"time is money." This presupposes a major link between efficiency and profitability and instills an economic relationship that operates across all organizational functions. The logical conclusion to this discourse is that time, which has no economic base, creates a conflict, establishing family, care, holidays and leisure time as examples of potential tension as Gerson and Jacobs (2004) argue in their development of time divides. Time as a catalyst has led to debates over the gendered nature of time and the barriers this places on individuals, particularly women who have a family. Dex (2005) identifies 48 hours of work per week as the marker over which stress dramatically increases and that women aged between 36 and 45 years are the group that on average are the most time poor.

The discourses around work/life balance gain ground in academic and media circles as key terms and highlight how a manager's competitive relations at work combined with temporal competition can result in different experiences for men and women. *Work/life balance, married to the company, greedy organizations* and *quality family time* are all examples of discourses, which some managers find difficult to adequately address in their approach to work and management. Whether it is from a personal perspective of juggling work and home or managing the various demands of subordinates and their changing situations, hard choices may need to be made to meet the demands of all organizations.

Gender, Managers and Temporal Competition

Temporal competition is defined by Dennehy (2010) as the ways and means in which time, as a fixed resource, and a commodity, directly or indirectly, becomes a competitor for a manager both at work and outside work. The collision of work and time can, as Dennehy's (2010) study finds, present a number of scenarios where too often, prevailing male dominated norms of organizational structures, behaviours and attitudes populate the management landscape. Attempts to assimilate large numbers of women into the labour market; particularly women with dependent children has been constrained by static temporal structures (Himmelweit & Sigala, 2001; McRae, 2003). For example, an average working day remains static in terms of the time demanded by organizations i.e. *9 to 5,* Monday to Friday. This typical working week presents two conflicts for workers with care responsibilities and/or interests outside work. The first conflict is that the 24/7 society does not support childcare services nor support services like doctors and dentists which are available outside *normal* working hours as emergency services only. The second conflict, exaggerated by the first, is the often relentless pressure on individuals who seek to win against clock time by achieving all their tasks at work, at home and at leisure.

Working Long Hours

Citing a culture of long hours in organizations continues to act as a means of creating barriers for some women managers who for a variety of reasons, do not or cannot offer the same degree of visual commitment to their positions as their male counterparts (Blair-Loy, 2003). Accepting that overtime is demanded by many organizations is, for some managers, simply a necessity of their positional role. However managing a balance between organizational and positional demands and life outside work is not always as simple. For a variety of reasons including career progression, job enjoyment, and job insecurity some managers use *presenteeism* to demonstrate almost unconditional commitment to their work (Massey, 1995). Presenteeism is defined by Simpson (1998) as the extent to which managers remain at work when the demands of their job do not require it. As a competitive element, Simpson (1998) argues that presenteeism is more likely to be subscribed to by men and often develops from the top down in the organizational hierarchy thus embedding itself in the culture. Rutherford (2001) observes that some organizations use long hours as a fear tactic to motivate managers, potentially leading to internal competitions between managers to see who can work the most hours.

Dennehy (2010) found that women managers were the group most keenly aware of long hour's cultures pervading the organizations where they worked. While all the managers interviewed largely accepted the necessity of long hours as opposed to presenteeism, they did not accept, as Powell and Graves (2003) argue, that non-compliance would result in career suicide. However, what emerged from Dennehy's (2010) study was that when motherhood was the reason for increased adherence to regular hours, a different set of rules and responses was experienced or observed.

Juggling Commitments

The suggestion that the relationship between a manager and the organization has strong emotional components can indicate the depth of the cultural bind. One manager interviewed in Dennehy's (2010) study, Susan, observes how some women, she does not mention men - have found the responsibility of long hours beyond what they can commit to professionally. In response to this realization, she further observes how these women leave to find more acceptable working arrangements. In describing the relationship between the organization and the manager like a marriage, Susan suggests a level of commitment beyond merely a set of tasks to be delivered in return for a fixed financial reward. Discourses around work and time have a dominant strand of emotive language, *marriage and commitment, work to live not live to work, having it all,* and *career suicide.*

How time and gender overlap in organizational structures play a role in extending the impact for example, of working hours. As some organizations demand more emotional attachment, the demand for organizational commitment is high and the implication is for loyalty through good times and bad. There is, as the managers discussed in

Dennehy's (2010) study, trouble with such a demand as they perceive and experience how the relationship is not necessarily equal between the individual and the organization.

Navigating time to satisfy the varying and changing components of a manager's life is complicated by such emotional references, as different demands and responsibilities become difficult to effectively prioritize (Adam, 2003). Engaging with temporal competition Dennehy's (2010) study argues begins with overcoming the following paradox. To understand time, one has to make time to think about one's relationship with time and all its associated components.

Working Practices

The practices associated with temporal competition often found embedded in organizational cultures may be so inherent that they go unchallenged. Exploring the practice of meetings Dennehy's (2010) study found that some managers appear to use tools such as scheduling early or late meetings to exercise degrees of authority over other people by placing specific demands on their time. How an individual manager structures their time at work during a day or week is influenced not only by the tasks they are required to complete, but also those involving interacting with other colleagues (Belbin, 2000).

For managers, time is a resource over which they may have limited control as the impact of superiors, peers, and subordinates can dominate daily schedules. A manager may be required to attend a meeting but have little or no control over the agenda or manner in which meetings are conducted. One senior manager interviewed in the Dennehy (2010) study, John, commented how meetings are often run by senior managers who are not necessarily skilled in the practice of efficient agenda driven meetings. Yet, because of their position, no one challenges their meeting processes, and the practices remain embedded. Making connections between time and the power to demand it from others, reinforces meetings as a platform where potentially gender and positional inequalities can be accentuated and where the battle for time can become a zero sum competition.

Being Busy: Different Meanings, Different Outcomes

Those individuals who regularly use the response *I'm so busy* as a response to any number of questions make it impossible to define busy as having just one meaning. This phrase is part of a popular discourse for working parents particularly that are familiar with the language of *double burdens, double shifts,* and *double days.* How women managers' with children particularly experience time, may as Dennehy's (2010) study suggests, be part of the performance they perceive society demands of them where a conflict between work and non-work time is implicit in the dual concept of care and career.

For example, Zoe, a mid-level manager, is honest about how the *I'm so busy* discourse is a useful tool which she uses to navigate certain areas of her life, using the widely understood lack of time as an excuse to justify personal and professional decisions and behaviours. Fran however admits to being frustrated by the *I'm so busy* discourse which, she suggests, should be a signal for people to relax and stop trying to compete with clock time. The competitive element of this battle with time has created a distraction from wider social issues such as women working while retaining the responsibility as primary caregivers. The myth of *having it all* may have changed to a reality of *doing it all* with women competing against the clock to see how many activities they can fit into 24-hours.

Another interviewee in Dennehy's (2010) study, Felicity, interestingly shared how her perception of time continues to be influenced by the attitudes and behaviour of people who dominate her working environment. Throughout her career, working more than *9 to 5* was regarded as normal and relative to how she defined busyness. In her current role however she has found that busyness is defined differently by the people she works with, and in her opinion, is markedly less frantic, when compared with other organizations. She is quick to comment how this new idea of busy combined with a prevailing culture of leaving on time and not feeling guilty, makes a positive contribution to her life. She further comments her team's productivity is not compromised, deadlines are met, and exceptions to working late are acceptable if they truly are exceptions.

Challenges Leading to Innovative Thinking

When discourses at work go unchallenged, the organizational cultures which foster and maintain them simply carry on. Gradually attitudes and behaviours are influenced and gain momentum as more people adhere to what is perceived and experienced as a normal organizational practice (Martin, 2003). How organizations present discourses around work and non-work time can offer insights into their dominant working cultures. Negotiating changes to the relationship between time and work may take root with some managers and their teams, but does not necessarily result in widespread application. *So how can organizations move successful pockets of new thinking forward in terms of temporal competition?*

First, as with all people-related polices, it is important to accept that *one size does not fit all.* Starting from a position that all workers are individuals and have needs that change over time - some predictable, some not - the front line representatives for the organizations and its policy implementation will be middle managers. This group described as the "clay layer" (Hochschild, 1997, p. 31) is increasingly being identified as the key to how innovative organizations can behave. Dennehy's (2010) study similarly found that while some managers expected their teams to experience various scenarios from having a family, outside interests, elder care responsibilities to retiring - other managers were caught in regimented and traditional attitudes of not bringing outside issues to work because they don't. What also emerges from the managers in Dennehy's study is how strongly they rely on their own experiences to formulate their implementation plans. For some managers, the holding up of role models by organizations or media as having resolved the issues of time were simply unbelievable and were, as the managers suggested, closely linked to the financial ability to buy services and, as a result, buy time.

Conclusion

The shift from gender equality metrics of equal pay and equal numbers of men and women in positions of power to the multiple dimensions of competition at work demonstrates how in using a different lens, new thinking can emerge. Temporal competition is arguably the most active dimension of the competition model since it has a relationship with all individuals. As a gateway to thinking about the other dimensions of competition, temporal competition itself presents an opportunity to think about how and why work time continues to be constructed within static parameters. The resonance of temporal competition with the managers in Dennehy's (2010) study is important telling the stories of managers' different experiences as they interact directly and indirectly with time and work. The organizational structures which perpetuate work time and clock time as a fixed resource, too often present temporal competition as a zero sum game where the organization embodies winning and individuals embody not winning. However, if the strategic aim of truly assimilating women into the labour market was founded on innovative approaches to temporal competition, organizations could create a new currency for measuring and delivering gender equality.

References

Adam, B. (2003). Reflexive modernization temporalized. *Theory, Culture, and Society, 20.*

Beck, U. (1992). *Risk analysis.* London, UK: Sage Publications.

Beck, U., & Beck Gersheim, B. (2002). *Individualization.* London, UK: Sage Publications.

Belbin, R., & Meredith, B. (2000). *Beyond the team.* Oxford, UK: Butterworth Heinemann.

Blair-Loy, M., & Jacobs, J. (2003). Globalization, work hours, and the care deficit among stockbrokers. *Gender and Society, 17*(2), 230–249.

Bradley, H. (1996). *Fractured identities.* Cambridge, UK: Polity Press.

Bradley, H. (1999). *Gender and power in the workplace.* Hampshire, UK: Macmillan Press Ltd.

Brannen, J., & Nilsen, A. (2005). Individualisation, choice and structure: A discussion of current trends in sociological analysis. *Sociological Review.*

Butler, J. (2004) *Undoing Gender.* Oxfordshire, UK: Routledge.

Connelly, S., & Gregory, M. (2008). Moving down: Women's part-time work and occupational change in Britain 1991–2001. *The Economic Journal,* 118(February): F52-F76.

Crompton, R. (1999). *Restructuring gender relations and employment.* Oxford, UK: Oxford University Press.

Dex, S., & Bond, S. (2005). Measuring work-life balance and its covariates. *Work Employment and Society, 19*(3).

Dennehy, J. (2010). *Gender and competition: A dynamic for managers.* (Unpublished doctoral dissertation). London School of Economics, England.

Edwards, P., & Wajcman, J. (2005) *The politics of working life.* Oxford, UK: Oxford University Press.

Gerson, K., & Jacobs, J. (2004). *The time divide: Work, family and gender inequality,* London, UK: Harvard University Press.

Himmelweit, S., & Sigala, M. (2004). Choice and the relationship between identities and behaviour for mothers with pre-school Children: Some implications for policy from a UK Study. *Journal of Social Policy 33*(3), 155–178.

Hochschild, A. (1997). *The time bind,* New York, NY: Henry Holt and Company.

Le Feurve, N. (1999). Gender, occupational feminization and reflexivity: A cross-national perspective. *Restructuring Gender Relations and Employment.* Oxford, UK: Oxford University Press.

Magretta, J. (2002). *What management is.* UK: Profile Books.

Martin, P. (2003) "Said and done" versus "saying and doing": Gendering practices, practicing G=gender at Work. *Gender and Society, 17*(3).

Massey, D. (1995). Masculinity, dualism, and high technology. *Trans Inst British Geographers* 20, 487–499.

McDowell, L. (1997). *Capital culture gender at work in the city.* Oxford, UK: Blackwell.

McRae, S. (2003). Constraints and choices in mothers' employment careers: A consideration of Hakim's Preference Theory. *British Journal of Sociology, 54*(3), 317–338.

Miner, H., & Longino, V. (1987). *Competition: A feminist issue.* New York, NY: The Feminist Press.

Mintzberg, H. (2004). *Managers not MBAs.* San Francisco, CA: Berret-Koehler Publishers Inc.

Oakley, A. (2000). *Experiments in knowing.* Cambridge, UK: Polity Press.

O'Connell Davidson, J., & Layder, D. (1994) *Methods, sex, and madness.* London, UK: Routledge.

Powell, G., & Graves, L. (2003) *Women and men in management.* London, UK: Sage.

Reich, R. (2000). *The future of success.* New York, NY: Alfred A Knopf.

Rifkin, J. (2004). *The European dream.* Cambridge, UK: Polity Press.

Rutherford, S. (2001). Are you going home already? *Time and Society, 10*(2/3), 259–276.

Schein, V. (2007). Women in Management: Reflections and projections. *Women in Management Review,* 22(1).

Simpson, R. (1998). Presenteeism, power, and organizational change: Long hours as a career barrier and the impact on the working lives of women managers. *British Journal of Management,* 9, S37-S50.

Wajcman, J. (1999). *Managing like a man.* Cambridge, UK: Polity Press.

About the Author

Having completed her undergraduate degree, A Bachelors of Arts Science (BA) in New Zealand, Dr. Jane travelled and settled in the United Kingdom. For 10 years, she worked in newspapers and digital media specializing in marketing and communications. Ready for her postgraduate work, Dr. Jane completed her Masters of Science (MS) in Gender Studies at Bristol University and returned to media marketing.

However, dissatisfied with not having found answers to questions around gender, management, and equality, Dr. Jane enrolled for a PhD at the Gender Institute of the London School of Economics. Here she conducted her doctoral research into how and in what ways competition is gendered for managers.

Dr. Jane is now using her expanded knowledge to work with organizations on developing strategies to gain competitive advantage from equality, compliance, and talent retention using marketing and communications.

To reach Dr. Jane for information on any of these topics, please email: dennehy65@googlemail.com

Assessing an Innovation: Student Outcomes from Master's Degree Programs in Organizational Leadership

Dr. Joseph W. T. Pugh

Actionable Knowledge for Decision Making

An organization that seeks to deploy and profit from an innovative product or service needs to develop a strategy for the deployment. The successful implementation of a strategy requires that the organization's performance, as well as that of the product or service, be assessed. Sound assessments require the compilation of both reinforcing and balancing feedback (Senge, 1990). From a body of feedback, an organization can distill actionable knowledge, meaning that the knowledge can be applied to situations in the real world (Argyris, 1996). The possession of actionable knowledge allows an organization to develop a body of best practices, to improve products and services, and to make informed decisions regarding future allocations of scarce resources.

How can the possession of actionable knowledge benefit an organization that seeks to develop a strategy for marketing innovative goods or services? Moreover, how can actionable knowledge be produced, especially when the service is intangible and the consumer base is not easily generalized? An example lays in the experiences of institutions of higher learning (IHL) that offer master's degree programs in the field of organizational leadership.

Over the last decade, an increasing number of institutions of higher learning (IHL) have deployed an innovative approach to graduate education, namely the establishment of master's degree programs devoted to the study and practice of organizational leadership. In a survey conducted in 2008, twenty-five directors of master's degree programs in organizational leadership reported on the methods that they employed to assess student outcomes from their programs and on the value of the knowledge produced by their assessment efforts (Pugh, 2009).

The Growth of Leadership Education

Writing in 1992, Conger described the study of leadership:

> This is the most exciting time to explore the issue of leadership development since the decade following World War II. Two important trends occurring over the 1970s and 1980s have produced a radical shift in the way we perceive leadership, and as a result, they have challenged traditional methods of teaching leadership. The first is a newfound *interest* in the idea of leadership itself. The second is an accompanying radical shift in what we know about the *process* of leadership. (p. 8)

One year after Conger's (1992) observations, Klenke (1993) noted the growing emphasis on the study of organizational leadership in graduate programs. That emphasis had by then manifested itself in nearly 800 higher education courses.

Within 10 years, that phenomenon had evolved into the establishment of graduate programs dedicated to the field of organizational leadership itself (Crawford, Brungart, Scott, & Gould, 2002). In a study conducted in 2001, Crawford et al. identified 37 institutions in the United States that offered master's degree programs in organizational leadership.

The desired student outcomes from a graduate degree program in organizational leadership are enhanced individual leadership abilities and, therefore, enhanced leadership performance (Kilgore, 2003; Poindexter, 2003; Srikanthan & Dalrymple, 2002). In this view, mere leadership literacy is not enough. To be successful, such programs must result in leadership competency. In other words, leadership degree programs ought to enable their graduates serve the needs of organizations and communities through their newly developed leadership abilities.

Crawford et al. (2002) also noted the non-traditional nature of the learners who enter such programs. They concluded that working adult learners seek educational programs that focus on the practical applications of leadership theories and models to professional activities. Several researchers argued that the development of such competencies involve complex learning processes. Flumerfelt et al. (2007) contended that the development of leadership abilities is not merely a series of training products, but an amalgamation of interconnected, transformative attitudes and behaviors that result from learning experiences.

The Higher Education Accountability Movement

Despite the growing emphasis on the assessment of educational outcomes during the last decade, a study conducted in 2000 by the National Center for Public Policy and Higher Education found insufficient evidence in any of the United States to evaluate the effects of college on students (Kuh, 2001). Peterson and Einarson (2001) acknowledged the wealth of literature providing outcomes assessment prescriptions but found that educational institutions did not engage in systematic research of their own management practices as part of their student assessment programs. Similarly, Burkhardt and Schoenfeld (2003) argued that research into educational topics seldom yielded practical solutions. They argued that the field of education had failed to leverage research-based assessment tools and processes commonly used by practitioners in the private sector. The United States Department of Education's Strategic Plan (2002) noted similar cause for concern. The report stated that the field of higher education is vulnerable to management fads and appeared to be unable to leverage scientific methods for collecting objective data for policy and decision-making.

An institution of higher learning seeks to satisfy the demands of learners and the community. After studying outcomes assessment of undergraduate accounting programs, Apostolou (1999) asserted that higher education has a variety of constituents, including industry, federal, state, and local governments, education accrediting bodies, parents, faculty, and students. Pringle and Mitchell (2007) argued that those stakeholders demanded that higher education provide an accounting for the money invested in higher education by showing evidence of learning on the part of students, and not just teaching on the part of educators.

A learner in a graduate degree program is both a consumer and a product (Douglas, Douglas, & Barnes, 2006; Rapert et al., 2004; Sirvanci, 1996, 2001). As a consumer, the learner exchanges tuition payments for meaningful learning experiences. The importance of such learning experiences may be the credential itself; the knowledge and abilities gained from the program; personal enrichment; or some combination.

The individual so educated then becomes the product demanded by the second consumer group, the community. Industry, governments, associations, community organizations, and schools all seek educated, capable individuals who can collaborate with other individuals to accomplish organizational goals. Karayaka and Karayaka (1996, as cited in Apostolou, 1999) argued that a focus on organizational needs is critical to an institution's success in a buyers' market in which prospective students will choose institutions that can make them viable competitors for job opportunities. Glazer-Raymo (2005) argued for the redesign of master's degree programs to better satisfy organizational requirements. Increased competition among institutions of higher education and the complex demands for human capital from businesses and industries operating in a global economy were the driving forces behind the redesign proposal.

Noting the emergence of graduate degree programs specifically designed to explore the theoretical bases of leadership in organizations, Heifetz (2000) called for substantive research into the practice of organizational leadership education. Collins (2001) argued that the field of leadership development suffered from "a deficiency of real scholarly knowledge" [and concluded that] "well-designed, thoroughly-reported empirical studies are needed to provide the necessary data to support that leadership development programs truly enhance organizational effectiveness" (p. 53).

A concomitant to the growth of graduate programs in organizational leadership has been the increasing emphasis on measuring the outcomes of higher educational programs. That emphasis has become known as the accountability movement in higher education (Huisman & Currie, 2004; Reville, 2006). Dannenbring (1996) asserted that the purpose of examining the outcomes of educational programs is to provide the information required by the efforts to improve those programs. McGourty (2000) pointed out that the increased emphasis on student outcomes assessment sprang from the concerns of industry and academic accreditation organizations that assessment efforts should include a wider array of student outcomes. Rapert et al. (2004) argued that the student is the primary consumer of educational programs and called for outcomes assessments that are based on student perceptions of quality and performance.

Conceptual Framework of the 2009 Pugh Study

At the core of this study was the concept of actionable knowledge. Argyris (1996) defined actionable knowledge as "knowledge that possesses external validity" (p. 390), meaning knowledge that can be applied to actual situations. Argyris posited that the purpose of actionable knowledge is not to predict conditions, but to create the conditions or changes that the knowledge indicates can be created (1998, as cited in Fullmer & Keys, 1998). Actionable knowledge from a degree program ought to allow learners to take theories, concepts, and models of organizational leadership espoused by their instructors and apply those to organizational situations. Actionable learning experiences are successful when learners are able to replicate in the real world those conditions that their instructors' models assert can be replicated.

Actionable knowledge from a higher education program is manifested in student outcomes. Student outcomes are the capabilities that a student or graduate gains from a higher education experience. Those capabilities may be knowledge and skills, or the consequences of knowledge, such as attitudes and behavior patterns, which can be applied in organizational settings (James Madison University, 2003).

In a study of student expectations from MBA programs, Rapert et al. (2004) noted a tendency among learners in graduate programs toward holistic educational programs that employ a variety of learning experiences that reach beyond the classroom environment. Scully (1988), argued that educational institutions are increasingly evaluated according to the benefits that they provide to businesses, organizations, and communities through the abilities of their graduates. Adrian and Palmer asserted that measures of quality in higher education should also encompass workplace capabilities such as intuition, leadership, and interpersonal communications, as well as operational skills (1999, as cited in Rapert et al., 2004).

Student learning is not the only actionable knowledge that can come from an educational program. Information about student outcomes is another form of actionable knowledge, one that is meaningful to the institution itself. The assessment by the institution of the outcomes from their programs must provide administrators with actionable knowledge that can be applied to decision-making and future program innovations. Student outcomes assessments can produce actionable knowledge, that is, knowledge about the processes and experiences that produced the outcomes. That knowledge can be of value in making decisions about and taking actions regarding current practices in organizational leadership education. Moreover, such knowledge can guide implementation of future program innovations.

Nature of the 2009 Pugh Study

The central question of this study was based on the evolution of leadership education and the growing demands for accountability in higher education: What methods are being employed by institutions in the United States that offer master's degrees in organizational leadership in order to measure the student outcomes from those master's programs?

To address the question, this researcher devised a descriptive, non-experimental, cross-sectional study, utilizing a mixed method research design (Creswell, 2003; Tashakkori & Teddlie, 2003; Greene, Caracelli, & Graham, 1989). In addition to exploring the methods used by institutions to assess the student outcomes from their master's degree programs in organizational leadership, the 2009 Pugh study sought to determine what findings those methods have yielded about student outcomes and how those findings were being used to make decisions.

The mixed method design used a survey to elicit responses that were descriptive of the assessment processes and techniques used by organizational leadership program directors to gauge student outcomes from their programs. The invitees for the survey were 103 leadership degree program directors who represented 95 institutions conducting 103 master's degree programs at 125 locations in 32 states in the United States. The numbers of programs and directors are coincidental. Four institutions conducting multiple programs identified a single director. Three institutions offering only one program at multiple locations identified a director for each campus.

Data was gathered for the 2009 Pugh study through the use of a 22-question survey instrument, posted on an Internet site hosted by a survey software provider. The survey was conducted in April 2008. The 103 survey invitees were identified by name, resulting in what the American Association for Public Opinion Research (AAPOR) classifies as an Internet survey of specifically named persons (AAPOR, 2008).

The mixed method survey questionnaire designed for this project utilized concurrent data procedures. Under the concurrent strategy, the current research study collected quantitative and qualitative data at the same time, and integrated them into an overall set of findings.

Findings Relative to Actionable Knowledge

The 2009 Pugh study revealed that institutions that offer master's programs in organizational leadership have been able to produce actionable knowledge, both through their programs and about their programs. The learning experiences in their programs have produced actionable knowledge for their learners. A majority of the survey respondents (n=21) reported that their assessments revealed that the graduates of their programs considered specific program content and experiences to have been effective in improving their leadership skills. Specifically:

1. 76.2% of programs noted that classroom discussions were considered to have been beneficial.

2. 71.4% of programs found that leadership theories were considered to have been instrumental in improving leadership abilities.

3. 66.7% noted that team projects were considered to have been instrumental in leadership ability improvements.

4. 66.7% reported that graduates saw research projects and reports as having been effective.

5. 38.1% of programs learned that case studies were considered to have been effective.

6. 33.3% of programs noted that course assessments were seen as having been helpful components of their program.

7. 23.8% of programs indicated that portfolios were seen as having been effective in improving the leadership skills of their graduates.

8. 19% reported that role-playing was considered by graduates to have been effective.

9. 14.3% of programs indicated that simulations were a significant factor.

Further evidence of actionable knowledge imparted by program learning activities came from reports of the specific leadership abilities that were reported to have been improved.

1. 81% reported increased skills in team leadership.

2. 71.4% of programs indicated that their graduates have reported improvements in work relationships.

3. 71.4% of programs reported learners' perceptions of improvements in communication and presentation skills.

4. 61.9% reported improved ability to handle ethical concerns.

5. 47.6% noted improvements in learners' training and coaching skills.

6. 38.1% reported feedback indicating improved skills in handling conflicts.

The data also indicate that the institutions that participated in the survey have produced actionable knowledge about their programs. Of the respondents, 20 of the 25 (80.0%) described improvements they had made to their programs that were initiated based on information that they had obtained from their outcomes assessments.

1. Courses have been added or expanded

2. Complete redesign of the program

3. The program now includes more hybrid courses with on-line availability.

4. Assessment feedback helped to shape the program's Strategic Plan

5. Change in required classes

6. Change in required thesis hours

7. Made program modifications

8. A master's program in leadership was changed to an MBA. The change was studied in the thesis of one of the program's learners.

9. New majors within the program were developed.

10. The order of courses was revised.

11. The program curriculum was redesigned.

12. Most students work full time and have families; they wanted more online course work and weekender programs.

13. A retreat was added to the program. (Pugh, 2009)

Development of the list of IHLs for the survey revealed that a significant growth sector in the graduate-level study of organizational leadership programs is in the MBA arena. Crawford et al. (2002) listed two institutions that offered an MBA program with an organizational leadership concentration. (One institution is a for-profit organization and was not included in this study.) Of the 95 institutions identified for this study, twelve offer MBA programs, either with a leadership concentration, or in an integrated, dual-degree program with a master's degree in leadership. One institution offers a master's degree in leadership, an MBA with a leadership concentration, and a dual degree program that integrates both. Two institutions offer executive MBA programs with leadership concentrations.

In addition to reported program changes, four respondents (19.04%) reported that assessment data led them to decide to not implement changes to their programs that they had contemplated making. For example, one respondent indicated that the institution had decided not to offer their master's program fully on-line. Another institution examined the matter of accepting transfer credits and decided not to accept credits from schools that the institution did not recognize.

Recommendation: Build Communities of Practice

Academia is not the only sector that faces the challenge of accountability for the value of leadership education. Wiessner and Sullivan (2007) asserted that organizations that implement professional development programs must demonstrate the benefits of those programs to their stakeholders. To do this, organizations need to "determine and then report whether the anticipated training outcomes have been achieved and whether there is a return on investment" (para. 16). The literature review for the 2009 Pugh study noted several authors who have argued that that academia in general has failed to demonstrate a sense of urgency in demonstrating those returns. Nirenberg (2003) asserted that degree programs in the field of management do not provide sufficient practical learning experiences in organizational leadership, even in those programs that provide adequate education in leadership theories. Allio (2005), called for development of new metrics for assessing leadership competency.

Bukowitz, Williams, and Mactas (2004) reported that business and industry—key stakeholders in organizational leadership degree programs—have also had difficulty producing tangible evidence of leadership development. Leadership is an intangible asset, commonly classified as human capital. Hernez-Broome and Hughes (2004) noted that even though companies such as PepsiCo and Johnson and Johnson expended appreciable amounts of time and resources to quantify the benefits of their leadership development initiatives, their efforts failed to produce definitive findings. The lack of precise data led some executives in those firms to question the effectiveness of their leader development programs. Creelman and Ulrich (2007) asserted that 29 Fortune 100 companies had poor human-capital information reporting practices.

One reason for the shortfall is the difficulty in measuring the contributions of an organization's intangible assets to the organization's performance. Another reason is the difficulty of factoring those contributions into traditional financial performance calculations. Bukowitz et al. (2004) and Fitz-enz (2006) asserted that human resource accounting requires data that is not readily discernible, and that the costs of developing an effective data-gathering infrastructure are high. The return side of the accounting equation is been fully understood by financial and human resource practitioners. Organizational decision-making can be severely constrained if precise information about leadership development outcomes is lacking (Bukowitz et al., 2004; Fitz-enz, 2006).

Clearly, academia and industry share the same challenges and frustrations in developing organizational leaders. To synergistically address those challenges, this researcher recommends that institutions that offer degree programs in organizational leadership partner with private and public sector organizations. These partnerships should create communities of practice to achieve common goals in leader and leadership development, particularly in demonstrating the benefits of leadership training and education. Communities of practice are social and organizational structures that are formed by practitioners who interact on a regular basis in order to share existing knowledge, address common concerns, and collaborate on the production of new knowledge (Argyris, 2004; Brown & Duguid, 1991; Elkjaer, 2004; Wenger, 2004; Wiessner & Sullivan, 2007). Communities of practice can produce new knowledge by sharing explicit and tacit knowledge, conceptualizing new models for organizational practice, and applying and assessing those models in organizational contexts (Wiessner & Sullivan).

The academy-industry synergy recommended above would have the potential to leverage the talents, frameworks, and practices of both sectors in developing models for human capital accounting (Ulrich, 2007). Ulrich and Smallwood (2005) noted the difficulty in communication between the two areas and challenged Human resource [HR] professionals to become conversant in financial concepts and practices to "directly connect to the thinking patterns of business leaders" (p 139). In an earlier work, Ulrich and Smallwood (2003) called for a dialog that seeks to connect human capital with shareholder value. Human resource managers need to effectively communicate the value of intangibles to corporate executives, who in turn can communicate the value of those intangibles to the firm's investors.

The academic partners in the community could facilitate a dialog between two key organizational constituencies in human capital development: human resource development (HRD) and financial management. Institutions of higher education can add value by contributing their knowledge of research methodologies and frameworks for analysis. Hatcher, Wiessner, Storberg-Walker, and Chapman (2006) argued that HRD educators could bridge the gap between theory and practice. Because of their unique perspectives on the junctures between HRD models and practices, Ulrich and Smallwood (2005) posited that HR educators and practitioners can be the designers of intangible audit models that can assess and improve on investments in intangible assets. Finally, leadership educators can act as honest brokers in assessing human capital initiatives. Hatcher et al. (2006) stressed that members of HRD communities of practice must question the status quo—theirs and the organization's—with a view toward the advancement of organizational learning and development.

The core for those communities of honest brokers exists in the adjunct faculty of organizational leadership master's programs. The survey responses reflected a heavy reliance on adjunct faculty by institutions that offer those master's programs. Six of the twenty-five survey respondents stated that adjunct instructors comprised 75% or more of their program faculty. Half of the survey respondents reported that at least 50% of their program faculty consisted of adjuncts. Those faculty members operate in the same work environments as their adult learners and their business and industry stakeholders. They embody the synergy of scholarship and practice. Just as adjunct instructors bring current organizational experience to the classroom (Banachowski, 1997; Haeger, 1998), they can bring their experience, perspectives, and practitioner networks to communities of practice, in order to improve the production of actionable knowledge for the development and implementation of educational strategies.

Conclusions

The research study summarized in this chapter revealed that institutions that offer master's programs in organizational leadership have been able to produce actionable knowledge, both through their programs and about their programs. The learning experiences in their programs have produced actionable knowledge for their learners. A majority of the survey respondents (n=21) reported that their assessments revealed that the graduates of their programs considered specific program content and experiences to have been effective in improving their leadership skills. Further evidence of actionable knowledge imparted by program learning activities came from reports of the specific leadership abilities that were reported to have been improved.

The data from the study also indicate that the institutions that participated in the survey have produced actionable knowledge about their programs. Twenty of the twenty-five respondents (80.0%) described twenty-nine improvements they had made to their programs that were initiated based on information that they had obtained from their outcomes assessments.

Innovation requires strategy. Strategy requires innovative implementation. Successful implementation requires rigorous assessment and detailed feedback. This is especially true in graduate education, where competition continues to grow for a share of a market consisting of information literate learners. Innovation strategies in higher education must include provisions for proving value to a variety of stakeholders, and not just potential students. Those strategies must also include mechanisms for innovative, continuous program and process improvements. Academia can increase its potential for successful strategy implementation by establishing communities of practice focused on discovering and disseminating best practices in leadership education.

References

Allio, R. (2005). Leadership development: Teaching versus learning. *Management Decision, 43*(7/8), 1071–1078.

American Association for Public Opinion Research (AAPOR). (2008). *Standard definitions: Final dispositions of case codes and outcome rates for surveys* (5th ed.). Lenexa, KS: AAPOR.

Apostolou, B. (1999). Outcomes assessment. *Issues in Accounting Education, 14*(1), 177–97.

Argyris, C. (1996). Actionable knowledge: Design causality in the service of consequential theory [Electronic version]. *The Journal of Applied Behavioral Science, 32*(4), 390–406.

Argyris, C. (2004). Reflection and beyond in research on organizational learning. *Management Learning; 35*(4), 507–509.

Banachowski, G. (1997). Advantages and disadvantages of employing part-time faculty in community colleges. *ERIC Digest.* (ERIC Document Reproduction Service No. ED405037).

Brown, J., & Duguid, P. (1991). Organizational learning and communities of practice: Toward a unified view of working, learning, and innovation. *Organization Science, 2*(1), 40–58.

Bukowitz, W., Williams, R., & Mactas, E. (2004). Human capital measurement: The centrality of people to knowledge-intensive organizations makes it important to measure the ROI on human capital. *Research-Technology Management, 47*(3), 43–49.

Burkhardt, H., & Schoenfeld, A. (2003). Improving educational research: Toward a more useful, more influential, and better-funded enterprise [Electronic version]. *Educational Researcher. 32*(9), 3–14.

Collins, D. (2001). Organizational performance: The future focus of leadership development programs. *The Journal of Leadership Studies, 7*(4), 43–54.

Conger, J. (1992). *Learning to lead: The art of transforming managers into leaders.* San Francisco, CA: Jossey-Bass.

Crawford, C., Brungart, C., Scott, R., & Gould, L. (2002). Graduate programs in organizational leadership: A review of programs, faculty, costs, and delivery methods. *Journal of Leadership Studies. 8*(4), 64–74.

Creelman, D., & Ulrich, D. (2007). Intangible value. *Leadership Excellence, 24*(4).

Creswell, J. (2003). *Research design: Qualitative, quantitative, and mixed methods approaches* (2nd ed.). Thousand Oaks, CA: Sage.

Dannenbring, G. (1996). *Monitoring educational outcomes: Information for decision-making and programmatic improvement.* Des Moines, IA: Mountain Plains Regional Resource Center. (ERIC Document Reproduction Service No. ED420139).

Douglas, A., Douglas, J., & Barnes, B. (2006). The student as customer. *Proceedings of the 9th Toulon—Verona Conference on Excellence in Services, Paisley, UK, 291–303.*

Elkjaer, B. (2004). Organizational learning: The 'third way.' *Management Learning, 35*(4), 419–434.

Fitz-Enz, J. (2006). Evaluating talent investments. *Leadership Excellence, 23*(6), 20.

Flumerfelt, S., Ingram, I., Brockberg, K., & Smith, J. (2007). A study of higher education student achievement based on transformative and lifelong learning processes. *Mentoring & Tutoring, 15*(1), 107–118.

Fullmer, J., & Keys, B. (1998). A conversation with Chris Argyris: The father of organizational learning. *Organizational Dynamics, 27*(2), 381–395.

Greene, J., Caracelli, V., & Graham, W. (1989). Toward a conceptual framework for mixed-method evaluation designs. *Educational Evaluation and Policy Analysis, 11*(3), 255–274.

Glazer-Raymo, J. (2005). *Professionalizing graduate education: The master's degree in the marketplace.* (Association for the Study of Higher Education Higher Education Report, Vol. 31, No. 4). San Francisco, CA: Jossey-Bass.

Haeger, J. (1998). Part-time faculty, quality programs, and economic realities. In D. W. Leslie (Ed.). *The growing use of part-time faculty: Understanding causes and effects* (pp. 81–88). San Francisco, CA: Jossey-Bass.

Hatcher, T., Wiessner, C., Storberg-Walker, J., & Chapman, D. (2006). How a research conference created new learning: a case study. *Journal of European Industrial Training, 30*(4), 256–271.

Heifetz, R. (2000). Leadership research. In Kellerman, B. & Matusak, L. R., eds. *Cutting edge: Leadership 2000.* College Park, MD: James MacGregor Burns Academy of Leadership.

Hernez-Broome, G., & Hughes, R. (2004). Leadership development: Past, present, and future. *Human Resource Planning, 27*(1), 24–32.

Huisman, J., & Currie, J. (2004). Accountability in higher education: Bridge over troubled water? *Higher Education 48*(4), 529–551.

James Madison University. (2003). *Dictionary of student outcome Assessment.* Retrieved from http://people.jmu.edu/yangsx/Search.asp?searchText=student+outcomes&submit=Search&Option= Definition

Kilgore, D. (2003). Planning programs for adults. *New Directions for Student Services, 102,* 81–88.

Klenke, K. (1993). Leadership education at the great divide: Crossing into the 21st Century. *Journal of Leadership Studies. 1*(1), 111–128.

Kuh, G. (2001). Assessing what really matters to student learning [Electronic version]. *Change, 33*(3), 10–17.

McGourty, J. (2000). Using multisource feedback in the classroom: A computer-based approach. *Institute of Electrical and Electronics Engineers Transactions on Engineering Education, 43*(2), 120–124.

Nirenberg, J. (2003). Toward leadership education that matters [Electronic version]. *Journal of Education for Business, 79*(1), 6–10.

Peterson, M., & Einarson, M. (2001). What are colleges doing about student assessment? *The Journal of Higher Education, 72*(6), 628–669.

Poindexter, S. (2003). The case for holistic learning. *Change, 35*(1), 24–30.

Pringle, C., & Mitchell, M. (2007). Assessment Practices in AACSB-accredited schools. *Journal of Education for Business, 82*(4), 202–211.

Pugh, J. (2009). *Methods used for the assessment of student outcomes from master's degree programs in organizational leadership.* (Doctoral dissertation). Retrieved from ProQuest Digital Dissertations database. (Publication No. AAT 339349).

Rapert, M., Smith, S., Velliquette, A., & Garretson, J. (2004). The Meaning of Quality: Expectations of Students in Pursuit of an MBA. *Journal of Education for Business, 80*(1), 17–24.

Reville, P. (2006). Coming soon to a college near you: Accountability. *Connection: The Journal of the New England Board of Higher Education 20*(5), 19–20.

Scully, J. (1988). A perspective on the future: What business needs from higher education. *Change 20*(2), 41.

Senge, P. (1990). *The fifth discipline: The art and practice of the learning organization.* New York, NY: Doubleday.

Sirvanci, M. (1996). Are students the true customers of higher education? *Quality Progress, 29*(10), 99–102.

Sirvanci, M. (2001). TQM issues in higher education. *Proceedings of the 6th World Congress for Total Quality Management, St. Petersburg, 1,* 598–603.

Srikanthan, G., & Dalrymple, J. (2002). Developing a holistic model for quality in higher education. *Quality in Higher Education, 8*(3), 215–224.

Tashakkori, A., & Teddlie, C. (Eds.). (2003). *Handbook of mixed methods in social & behavioral research.* Thousand Oaks, CA: Sage Publications.

Ulrich, D. (2007). Dreams: Where human resource development is headed to deliver value. *Human Resource Development Quarterly, 18*(1), 1–8.

Ulrich, D., & Smallwood, N. (2003). Building intangible value from the outside In. *Leader to Leader, 2003*(28), 24–30.

Ulrich, D., & Smallwood, N. (2005). HR's New ROI: Return on intangibles. *Human Resource Management, 44*(2), 137–142.

United States Department of Education. (2002). *Strategic Plan 2002–2007.* Retrieved from www.ed.gov/about/reports/strat/plan2002–07/index.html

Wiesener, C., & Sullivan, L. (2007). Constructing knowledge in leadership training programs. *Community College Review, 35*(2), 88–112.

Wenger, E. (2004, Jan/Feb). Knowledge management as a doughnut: Shaping your knowledge strategy through communities of practice. *Ivey Business Journal Online, 1.*

About the Author

Dr. Joseph W. T. Pugh holds a Bachelor of Science (BS) in Political Science from Drexel University; a Master of Arts (MA) in Management and Human Relations from Webster University; a Master of Business Administration (MBA) from Averett University; and a Doctorate of Management (DM) in Organizational Leadership from University of Phoenix School of Advanced Studies.

Dr. Joseph is an Associate Professor of Business Administration at Immaculata University, where he teaches Organizational Leadership, Business Law, and Management Information Systems as well as being the faculty moderator of the Immaculata chapter of Sigma Beta Delta, the business and management honor society. He is a retired U.S. Army officer. His experience includes several assignments in the field of education and training management.

A native of Philadelphia, PA, Dr. Joseph currently resides in Haddonfield, NJ with his wife Anne.

Additional published works include his dissertation: *Methods Used for the Assessment of Student Outcomes from Master's Degree Programs in Organizational Leadership* and the facilitators' and learners' guides for Immaculata University's courses in *Business Law* and *Issues in Management.*

To contact Dr. Joseph for further information on his research, please send an e-mail to jpugh@immaculata.edu

Change Models and 21st Century Organizations: An Epistemic Journey to Creative Innovation

Dr. Beverly D. Carter
& Dr. Beverly Hernandez

Creative Innovation and the History of Organizational Change

The twenty first century organization is intensely poised for transition. In the wake of global economic disasters, environmental chaos, political upheaval, dishonesty in business and frightening, massive fundamental changes in our healthcare system, organizations are being challenged to creatively innovate a future for the highest good of the communities they serve. The world is faced with an uncertain future demanding that organizations, societal microcosms purge themselves of outmoded thinking and old behaviors that no longer serve the common good. The impact of these and other overwhelming problems has been felt around the world forcing many organizations to change their operating procedure models and adapt their organizational intelligence to creativity and innovation. As a result of being thrown into new circumstances many organizations stand on the precipice of necessary reform where leaders are challenged not to survive, but to learn new ways to find opportunities to thrive in business.

The topic of organizational change never seems to go away. Workplace change has a long history that presents at the core of the entire discipline of organizational development, and it holds prominence in the historical discourse of organizational behavior, organizational theory, and leadership strategies. Most contemporary organizations face an environment framed by rapid economic growth, emerging new technologies, and changing market requirements in an expanding, competitive global economy (Hatch, 1997; Morgan, 1997; Perrow, 1993). The dramatic impact of transformative processes on organizational practices presents both opportunity and threat to contemporary leadership. The rules of economic engagement have changed, creating an imperative for leaders to alter their environments to more effectively compete in this new economy.

Postindustrial leaders are called to initiate strategies that satisfy the requirements of these turbulent times. Jack Welch, of General Electric, Mitchell Kertzman of Powersoft, and Mike Harper of ConAgra are examples of leaders who successfully lead change efforts. In difficult times these leaders used knowledge and creativity to establish sustainability within their respective organizations. Such initiators of evolutionary practices continue to investigate and embrace opportunities that promote renewal, sustain change efforts, and transform organizations into relevant, effective economic engines.

The following paragraphs not only discuss the history of change

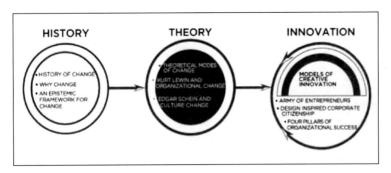

Figure 1: Life Cycle of Creative Innovation

but also decipher the epistemic applicability of change (see Figure 1). These paragraphs unveil specific and significant models of change generated by recognized theorists and thinkers such as Kurt Lewin and Edgar Schein whose critical contributions add value to the organizational change literature, which established the foundation for creative innovation.

History of Change

Historical evaluation of how organizations behave as they interact with their internal and external environment reveals much about the organizational change phenomenon. The charted history of organizational change exposes leadership interest in transformation as a constant reality as far back as 535 BC when Heraclitus was described as the 'great philosopher of eternal change' (Kirk, Raven, & Schofield, 1995). Heraclitus likened the change phenomenon to the flow of a river that regenerates itself through constant renewal (Kirk et al., 1995). A cursory review of contemporary literature positions organizational change as the historical reconstruction, transformation, invention and reinvention of the work system within organizational societies (Hatch, 1997; Morgan, 1997; Shafritz & Ott, 2001). Organizations once functioned under the authority of a single leader. Over time, the expansion of power structures has been revealed by established boards, and stakeholders who belong to centerless organizations (Hesselbein, Goldsmith, & Beckhard, 1997). From past systems within the industrial revolution, transition from an agricultural society to an industrial economy; from early systems of subcontracting, the creation of textile mills and steel factories, through the post-industrial development of complex computer systems and information technologies, change has been central to the organizational experience (Dawson, 2003; Shafritz & Ott, 2001).

Dawson (2003) described the authoritarian industrial entrepreneurs as those change agents who determined the type, speed, and direction of change in an environment where employees had little or no input regarding the changes imposed upon them. The rapids of change spawned Taylorism that birthed new leadership practices which eroded worker solidarity as organizations began to be conceived as a network of human parts (Morgan, 1997). Principles of Taylorism dehumanized workers, requiring them not to think, but rather to use their manpower. Yet the unprecedented productivity and wealth that accompanied Taylor's influential scientific management change initiative to standardized, best methods remained attractive to economic and organizational leaders (Shafritz & Ott, 2001).

The rapid creation of new knowledge and the speed and availability of information resulted in the emergence of the post-industrial society (Hatch, 1997; Shafritz & Ott, 2001). This change to a post-industrial/postmodern environment resulted in global competition, flattened hierarchical structures, decentralization, flexible organizational designs, and celebration of uncertainty (Morgan, 1997; Shafritz & Ott, 2001). This organizational bias toward change is driven by strong visionary leadership that rewards inventive acts that favor renewal and maintain the organization's solvency.

Chaos theory has added to the rich and varied history of organizational change. Contemporary physicists consider change to be inextricably intertwined to human existence (Halligan, 2004). Chaos theorists have indicated that complex systems are influenced by different types of attractors. Some attractors draw systems into a state of equilibrium while other attractors have the propensity to flip a system into a completely new configuration (Morgan, 1997). Proponents of chaos theory contend that there is a unique rhythmic balance between order and chaos evident in the universe. Acceptance of this line of thought enables us to view chaos and order as significant aspects of the conflict that exists between old and new ways within organizations and the forces that upset this balance resulting in transformation (Halligan, 2004).

Why Change?

Shaffritz and Ott (2001) discussed the desire to become more socially and environmentally stable as being at the heart of organizational change. Commentators on the history and future of organizations critically emphasize the need to relinquish cherished assumptions and irrelevant, inefficient practices. These change leaders stress the necessity of the emergence of new knowledge to survive intense domestic and international competition (Dawson, 2003; Hesselbein et al., 1997; Kanter, 1992).

Change has become the one certainty within contemporary organizations (Dawson, 2003). One might conceive of the traditional organization as a silo system with the defining goal of stability in the face of socioeconomic, political, and technological changes. Historically, changes in these variables within society resulted in large scale changes at an organizational level. Conversely, new technologies open the gateway for inventive practices that encourage the creation of flexible organizations that can adapt to changing market demands (Kanter, 1992). Contemporary organizations struggle to find new ways to adapt to the remapping of the globe along with new and often unfamiliar markets on the global horizon. Organizations are challenged to purge inefficiencies and reengineer processes in order to gain a competitive advantage and remain solvent (Carr, Hard, & Trahant, 1996).

Today, organizational leaders recognize the need for a paradigm shift because previously held assumptions have either lost their relevance or have become outmoded. Postmodernist thinking considers these overturned assumptions as opportunities to add inventive strategies and alternatives that better position the organization. Contemporary organizations that apply postmodern thought are viewed as open, circular systems with porous walls that allow inventive practices and renewal to occur as they interact with the internal and external environment (McCauley, Moxley, & Van Veslor, 1998).

The current bias toward organizational change is based on the premise that the inability to change will result in the death of the organization. For this reason Kanter (1989) claimed that competitive organizations of the future should embrace strategic alliances, partnerships, and inventive practices in an emergent environment that successfully manages change. In this environment, leaders learn to master rather than become the victims of change. As new challenges and problems form due to changing technologies and market conditions, organizations need more flexible styles of organizing and managing (Morgan, 1997).

Organizational theorists suggest that flexible, chameleon-like organizational structures tend to ensure buoyancy through the rapids of change because they are continuously able to reposition themselves and amend work practices to effectively deal with change. Further contemporary trends encourage embracing knowledge workers, a diverse workforce, effective partnerships, delayering and outsourcing, and for the consistent adoption of new technology which imply the need for change (Dawson, 2003; Hesselbein et al., 1996).

Toward an Epistemic Framework for Change

The evolution of human knowledge with its influx of new information and advances in science and technology has spawned continual change. The critical and creative thinking strategies associated with new technology has placed information at the core of dramatic change within 21st century organizations. For this reason, Senge (1990) defined knowledge-based organizations as learning organizations where people continually enhance their ability to craft new inventive strategies for organizational survival. Nonaka and Nishiguchi (2001) contend that the emergence of new knowledge was the most contributory factor in the change invention strategies that helped Japanese companies maintain success, relevance, and a competitive edge. These solutions driven organizations applied the scientific method of knowledge acquisition, using inferential and hypothesis generating strategies to justify the application of change initiatives. Reason, logic, and objective thought are not abandoned in the change process but are used to conceptualize problems, form solutions, and submit predictions related to the invention of new processes within the organization.

The relevance of knowledge to functions of change within organizations is evidenced by the consistent need to apply problem resolution and knowledge creation to business environments that are unstable and consistently changing (Harvard Business Review, 1998). Postmodern advocates view the creation and use of knowledge as a means to emancipate rather than control and contemporary leaders value knowledge capital as it expands information, reduces error, and infers predictability (Hatch, 1997; Nonaka & Nishiguchi, 2001). Such epistemic justification promises consistent results, gives reasonable explanation, and submits probabilities related to the application of change strategies. Argyris (1996) supports this philosophy and offers knowledge as the central leader driven activity for creating change within 21st century business environments.

Theoretical Models of Change

Change is everywhere. It is a transformational process that requires inventive ways of thinking and behaving. For this reason, one might argue that there can never be a universal model of organizational change as processual change involves movement to a prospective position that is both uncertain and unknown (Dawson, 2003; Quinn 1996). The speed and availability of new information fuels the need for change in organized, systematic, predictable behaviors within organizations. The acceleration and velocity of change forces contemporary leaders to be ready for new realities as new realities mandate new leadership approaches (Harper, 1998).

The concepts of change and organizations are not always complementary. Change theory was initiated in part by modernist models of structured change process (Hatch, 1997). This view of change involved a leader change-agent that introduced transformation into the organization with some degree of deliberation. A change-centered perspective erodes stability-centered views and stands at odds with traditional classical management models of routinized organizational practices. Transformation as an imperative to thriving in 21st century environments invites leader acquaintance with change models that remain relevant to organizational function (Hatch, 1997; Quinn, 1996). The following discussion will focus on two distinct leader driven change models that provided noteworthy, insightful, contributions to understanding the change process within organizations. The following is a detailed synthesis, analysis, and critique of the change models presented by Kurt Lewin, Edgar Schein, and a look at three models of creative innovation.

Kurt Lewin and Organizational Change

Few people have had as significant an impact on the organizational change management literature as Kurt Lewin. He established one of the earliest and most extensively applied change process theories. Lewin's influence is pervasive in contemporary change management, training and development, work designs, leadership styles, and system change. His ingenuity and innovative experimental design were evident in the 'models' he created which still provide the basis for many current change management concepts (Levasseur, 2001; Wolf, 1992). The most profound of his innovative influential designs was his model of processual change in human systems (Levasseur, 2001; Schein, 1996). His classic change theories served as the genesis of a change model that inspired subsequent conceptualizations. The seminal nature of Lewin's change dictums gave relevant insight into how change occurs and enriched the management literature regarding the essential role of change agents within successful organizations (Hatch, 1997; Levasseur, 2001; Schein, 1996; Wolf, 1992).

Lewin was a humanitarian who believed that resolution to social conflict was infinitely connected to planned change. He believed such change would enhance human understanding and facilitate restructuring of human perception of the world around them (Burnes, 2004). Lewin's practical guide to change involved 4 elements: Field theory, Group dynamics, Action research, and the 3-step change model (Burnes, 2004; Hatch, 1997; Schein, 1996).

Group Dynamics

Infinitely humanistic, Lewin was the first psychologist to write about group dynamics and its relationship in shaping the behavior patterns of its members (Brunes, 2001; Schein, 1996). This element of Lewin's theory stressed that the main focus of effective change was related to the dynamics of group behavior rather than individual direction (Brunes, 2001; Hatch, 1997; Schein, 1996). Lewin contended that it was pointless to attempt individual change when individuals were constrained to conform to group pressures. Subsequently, he presented concentrated change strategies that focused at the level of the group in order to create disequilibrium and change (Schein, 1996).

Wolf (1992) described Lewin's work with a group he was assisting to change their eating habits. He used two methods to urge participants to change their ways. To one group he presented an authority lecture and the other was to have the participants discuss the matter and come up with a group decision. The research later revealed that those who participated in the group decision making changed their eating habits. Following Lewin's historic ground breaking group dynamics' philosophy, a wide-spread interest in group cohesion, structure, and decision was noted in the management literature (Wolf, 1992).

Action Research

To identify the active forces within and between groups, action research draws from field theory which directs management focus to the groups in which individuals interplay. It dovetails with the group dynamics element of Lewin's change model as it places emphasis on the importance of participative, collaborative processes among groups to realize effective change (Burnes, 2004). Lewin was concerned that even with these elements; change toward improved organizational performance might be short lived. For this reason, he established and presented his renowned 3-step model of change.

Lewin's 3-Step Change Model

Lewin instituted this 3-step change model as part of his elegant integrated approach to investigating, understanding, and implementing planned change (Brunes, 2004). According to this model, successful change involves 3 specific steps: unfreezing, change/movement, and refreezing (Burnes, 2004; Hatch, 1997; Schein, 1996).

Step 1: Unfreezing. Lewin postulated that unfreezing occurred by injecting additional forces for change into the field (Martinsons, 1996). It involved unfreezing the presenting equilibrium to create a new environment for change. Prior to discarding old behavior patterns and successfully adopting new ones, the equilibrium must be destabilized. Before leaders attempt to introduce a change, Lewin emphasized the need to create a situation where participants in the change would recognize the risks and shortcomings of continuing their current practices.

Step 2: Change stage/moving. Hatch (1997) perceived Lewin's change stage as influencing the strategic direction of a newly unbalanced system. Schein (1996) saw this stage as influencing learning but not necessarily controlling or predicting direction, while Martinsons (1996) described it as simply moving from the initial state to the new end state. It was Lewin's intent to integrate this stage with his Action Research based learning model to enable individuals within organizations to move (change), to a more acceptable set of behavior patterns (Brunes, 2004).

Step 3: Refreezing: The refreezing process requires some degree of congruence among group participants allowing norms, routines, and traditions to be transformed. It involves locking in the end state that has been achieved (Martinsons, 1996; Schein, 1996). In Lewin's model, refreezing occurs when a new quasi-stationary equilibrium is achieved and stabilized within the organization and becomes an institutionalized practice.

Edgar Schein and Culture Change

Edgar Schein pioneered the study of corporate culture change establishing theories that underpin the framework of the organizational culture change literature. As an internationally respected consultant Schein has made significant contributions to the corporate change literature clarifying and illuminating facets of culture and culture change within organizations (Dawson, 2003). Schein believed that every organization has a unique culture and the culture of an organization is among its most valued assets. H e simplified cultural complexities by describing life cycle stages in which organizations develop from infancy to potential death. He postulated that as an organization moves through its stages it develops skills, values, and competencies that allow the acquisition of additional resources. Organizations with the ability to acquire resources are likely to generate surplus resources that further enhance growth (Jones, 2001). Over time an organization can transform itself and become something different than it was when it started (Jones, 2001).

Schein (1997) suggested that the culture of an organization usually revolves around its leader as leaders embed the ideals that come to be common practice by everyone within the organization. For this reason changing corporate culture is a very complex, time consuming process, however, changes can be made to corporate culture in order to enhance organizational performance (Kotter & Heskett, 1992).

Schein's Model of Culture Change

Schein presented his own 3-stage model of transformative change within contemporary organizations. This 3-stage model involved (a) unfreezing and creating the motivation to change; (b) learning new concepts and learning new meanings for old concepts; and (c) internalizing new concepts and meanings.

Stage 1: Unfreezing—Creating the motivation to change (disconfirmation)

Schein (1996) suggested that all forms of learning and change started with dissatisfaction or frustration caused by experiences that disconfirm our expectations. These disconfirming forces included economic, political, moral, technological, or legal threats that serve as motivation to change existing practices within an organization. Schein also presented scandal as a powerful motivator for change. He also proffered the collision of cultures evident in mergers; acquisitions, joint ventures, and an organization's need to survive as obvious motivators for change. Schein (1999) discussed new leadership with a compelling vision and the acquisition of new information through education and training as powerful sources of disconfirmation.

Stage 2: Learning new concepts and new meaning for old concepts

Schein (1997) stated that new standards for evaluation, new concepts, and new meaning for old concepts could be learned through two basic mechanisms: (a) imitating a role model and having psychological identification with that role model, and (b) inventing a series of solutions until one works for the department or organization.

Forms of imitation and role modeling can be provided through bench marking, case studies, films, role-plays, and simulation (Schein, 1999). Schein (1997) cautions that this mechanism is best suited to organizations that clearly conceptualize and articulate the new direction and its methodologies, and also offers clarity regarding the performance requirements needed to succeed in the new environment.

Stage 3: Internalizing New Concepts

Schein (1999) described the internalization of new concepts by members of the organization as the final step in the transformative process. Internalizing new concepts signifies congruence between the new concept and the expectations, behavior, and personality of the learner (Schein, 1996). When new concepts meet the success expectations of the learner and significant others within the organization, then it stabilizes and these concepts become the new practices that frame the environmental culture.

3 Models of Creative Innovation

Today, organizations that are microcosms of society are challenged to embrace creative innovation and discard outdated modern and post modern practices. Creativity and innovation have become the prerequisites to establishing successful initiatives to maintain superior and long lasting performance. Organizations are ultimately encouraged to develop critical and creative thinking skills to address their mental models and build innovation and creativity into their DNA to thrive.

> Innovation comes not from some unique inspiration but from looking at the world in a different way. It comes from having a fresh perspective, an alternate way of seeing things, angle of view that lets you see through the familiar and spot the unseen. (Gibson & Waghorn, 2010, p. 1)

Surviving in business is tantamount to extinction without creativity and innovation as a critical leadership competency.

Current literature suggests a myriad of new change models for organizations in support of the successful use of creative innovation. A few of these models are: the Army of Entrepreneurs, Design-inspired corporate citizenship, and the four pillars of organizational success. The *Army of Entrepreneurs* is a leadership and management model that galvanizes the internal force of dedicated employees, in the guise of independent contractors, to use creativity and innovative methods to drive the new economy (Prosek, 2010).

A second change model introduces design-inspired corporate citizenship which is "all about seeing the world not simply as it is but as it could be" (Cooperrider, 2010, p. 24) which is the very nature of the field of design thinking. Change by design helps organizations capitalize on organizational creativity and innovation to generate business opportunities that benefit the world, by addressing social and global problems. This is done by creating "design visions, cultivating appreciative intelligence, rapid prototypes, feedback loops and iterative pathways imbedded within and increasingly uncertain and dynamic world" (Cooperrider, 2010, p. 27).

A third change model examines four pillars of organizational greatness through leadership, business culture, politics and reward structures. It encourages organizations to become *people-centric* as opposed to product or process-centric. This is accomplished by challenging hierarchal leadership and promoting leadership from where ever it is found within an organization. Leadership which is the first pillar is "demonstrated through a commitment to each other's accomplishments and the overall success of the organization" (Laurin, 2010, p. 26). The second pillar, business culture, allows for the creation of an environment that encourages employees to act like they own the business. This is accomplished by opening lines of communication at all levels of an organization with regard to proposed changes allowing for questions and challenges that may affect the viability of a proposed change. The third pillar, politics, asks if we live in a democratic society why would we choose to work in a dictatorship. The creation of a democratic model also known as the *corporate constitution* encourages an atmosphere where creativity and innovation can flourish. The fourth pillar supports the creation of a reward structure that matches the new view of leadership in a team-oriented culture with a democratic organizational culture (Laurin, 2010).

The desire to innovate is not enough. Many organizations have identified innovation as one of their top strategic priorities but have not yielded expected results. One reason companies struggle with incorporating creativity and innovation into their organization is that the process of being creative may not fit within the organizational design of these companies. For example, innovation is a process associated with management functions; however, managers are "encouraged to minimize risks and value predictability" ("Leader to Leader," 2004, p. 59).

The aim for organizations incorporating creative innovation techniques is threefold: first, it is to ensure that the managers are enabled to assume the risks associated with innovation, with the understanding that this may change the core beliefs and cultural values of the organization. Second, create a democratic working environment that encourages employees to feel like they are co-owners of the organization. This may shift a bureaucratic or autocratic environment to a democratic structure encouraging the freedom of thought and shared knowledge. Third, be sure that the reward structure utilized in your organization encourages thinking and actions that will propel innovation into your organization (Laurin, 2010).

Conclusion

The preceding section traversed the history of change, via the essential nature of change to human existence, and presented an epistemic framework as a rationale for its existence within contemporary organizations. The authors conducted a critical analysis, synthesis and critique of a wide range of referents. The selected change theories represent traditional and contemporary change models by renowned organizational theorists: Kurt Lewin, and Edgar Schein, as well as a few current models that encourage creative innovation. These models were discussed with regard to their utility, contribution, and relevance to contemporary change concepts within organizations. The change philosophies of these theorists have had a significant impact on leader/follower relationships within past and present organizations through the application of critical information, the creation of new knowledge, and the concept of value for employees (Hatch, 1997; Hesselbein et al., 1997). Their work has served to shape the thinking and practice of change as it occurs within organizations.

Albert Einstein stated, "We cannot solve our problems with the same thinking we used when we created them" (Rethmeir, 2010, p. 159). Contemporary theorists place change at the core of competitive advantage and the ultimate survival of organizations of the 21st century. Further, they announce the importance of having a blueprint for change that is adapted to the special needs of the organization (Carr et al., 1996). The fact that many change initiatives fail tells us that those organizations should critically appraise their selected model of change and method of introduction into the organizational culture (Dawson, 2003). Leaders are challenged to embrace the many uncharted faces of change that emerge from interactions with shrinking world markets and the knowledge that success may be brilliantly disguised as creative innovation.

References

Agryis, C. (1996). Actionable knowledge: Design causality in the service of consequential theory. *Journal of Applied Behavioral Science, 32*(4), 390–406.

Burnes, B. (2004). Kurt Lewin: The practical theorist for the 21st century. *Journal of Management, 1*(1), 31–37.

Cooperrider, D. (2010). Managing-as-designing in an era of massive innovation. *Journal of Corporate Citizenship, 24–33.*

Carr, D. K., Hard, K. J., & Trahant, W. J. (1995). *Managing the change process: A fieldbook for change agents, consultants, team leaders, and reengineering managers.* Ontario, Canada: McGraw-Hill Ryerson.

Dawson, P. (2003). *Understanding organizational change: The contemporary experience of people at work.* Thousand Oaks, CA: Sage.

Gibson, R., & Waghorn, T. (2010). *Four ways of seeing that set true innovators apart.* Retrieved from www.forbes.com/2010/04/15/innovation-four-keys-leadership-managing-creativity

Halligan, F. (2004). Metamorphosis: Change and continuity, chaos and order, conflict, and transformation. *Journal of Religion and health, 43*(3), 12–27.

Harper, S. (1998). Leading organizational change in the 21st century. *Journal of Industrial Manager, 40*(3), 1–10.

Hatch, M. J. (1997). *Organization theory: Modern, symbolic, and postmodern perspectives.* New York, NY: Oxford University Press.

Hesselbein, F., Goldsmith, M., & Beckhard, M. (Eds.) (1997). *Organizations of the future.* San Francisco, CA: Jossey-Bass.

Jones, G. (2001). *Organizational theory, design, and change* (4th ed.). Upper Saddle River, NJ: Prentice Hall.

Kanter, R. (1989). *When giants learn to dance: Mastering the challenges of strategy, management, and careers.* London, UK: Lenwin.

Kirk, G., Raven. J., & Schofield. M. (1995). *The prosocratic philosophers: A critical history with a selection of texts* (2nd ed.). New York, NY: Cambridge University Press.

Kotter, J. P., & Heskett, J. L. (1992). *Corporate culture and performance.* New York, NY: The Free Press.

Laurin, C. (2010). Something "fishy" about Boeing. *Journal for Quality & Participation. 25–27.*

Leader to Leader. (2004). *Bright ideas are not enough: From innovation to results.* 59–60.

Levasseur, R. (2001). People skills: Change management tools and Lewin's change model. *Interfaces, 35*(4), 71–74.

Martinsons, M. (1996). Cultural constraints on radical re-engineering: Hammer and Lewin meet Confucius. *Journal of Applied Management, 5*(1), 1- 8.

Morgan, G. (1997). *Images of organization.* San Francisco, CA: Sage Publications.

Nonaka, I., & Nishigushi, T. (2001). *Knowledge emergence.* New York, NY: Oxford University Press.

Perrow, C. (1986). *Complex organizations: A critical essay* (3rd ed.). New York, NY: McGraw Hill.

Prosek, J. (2010). *It takes an 'army of entrepreneurs' to build a business.* Retrieved from *www.forbes.com/2010/7/14/business-management-leadership-forbes-woman-entrepreneurs*

Quinn, R. (1996). *Deep change: Discovering the leader within.* San Francisco, CA: Jossey Bass.

Rethmeier, K. (2010). Innovation for healthcare reform: creating opportunities to explore, expand, and excel. *Journal of Management & Marketing in Healthcare, 3*(2) 150–162.

Schein, E. H. (1996). Kurt Lewin's change theory in the field and in the classroom: Notes toward a model of managed learning. *Systems Practice, 9*(1), 27–47.

Schein, E. H. (1997). *Organizational culture and leadership* (2nd ed.). San Francisco, CA: Jossey-Bass.

Schein, E. H. (1999). *The corporate culture survival guide.* San Francisco, CA: Jossey-Bass.

Senge, P. (1994). *The fifth discipline.* Retrieved from http://www.rtis.com/ nat/user/ jfullerton/review/learninghtm.

Shafritz, J. M., & Ott, J. S. (Eds.). (1997). *Classics of organization theory* (5th ed.). Upper Saddle River, NJ: Prentice-Hall.

Wolf, W. (1992). *Responsibility. Journal of Organizational Change Management, 5*(3), 1- 4.

About the Author

 New York author Dr. Beverly D. Carter holds several accredited degrees; a Bachelor of Arts (BA) in Psychology from Western New England College; a Master of Science (MS) in Adult Education Human Resources Management from Fordham University; and a Doctorate of Management (DM) in Organizational Leadership from University of Phoenix School of Advanced Studies.

Dr. Bev is a "corporate physician" with Business Prosperity Solutions where she serves organizations as a mentor and guide as they shift their organizational paradigms; Civil Servant dedicated to contract management, program development and monitoring of subcontracted, not for profit agencies; and volunteer consultant with Ejayes Charities which supports plans for medical missions to serve the underprivileged in Africa and most recently, Haiti.

Dr. Bev led the Older Driver Coalition to winning the 2009 Gold NACO award for exceptional development of a county government program for the development of a Roll Call Training for Law Enforcement as "first responders" to caregivers and the growing older driving community. She participated in the development of a County Government Publication: *A Guide for Caregivers* for which her department won the 2009 Bronze Achievement Award.

Additional published works include her dissertation: *The Impact of Thinking and Leadership Styles on the Advancement of Women and The Refractive Thinker Volume IV: Ethics, Leadership, and Globalization: Changing the Hegemonic Impact of Leadership Advancement for Women.*

To reach Dr. Beverly Carter for information on any of these topics, please e-mail: dr.beverlycarter@yahoo.com

About the Author

Dr. Beverly J. D Hernandez has been an innovative leader in the healthcare environment for more than 15 years. Her passion for learning fueled the completion of multiple degrees: A Bachelor of Science (BS) degree in Nutrition from Hunter College, A Masters of Science (MS) in Clinical Nutrition from New York University, (NYU) and an internship in Medical Nutrition Therapy through the Department of Medicine at the Bronx Veteran's Administration.

Dr. Beverly further pursued her doctoral degree (PhD) at Walden University in Applied Management and Decision Sciences with an emphasis on Leadership and Change. Her remarkable academic career demonstrates her commitment to healing and caring for ailments that afflict the success of human systems.

As part of her commitment to social change, Dr. Beverly serves as nutrition spokesperson for television and radio programs requiring expert nutrition opinion, served as board member of the American Dietetic Association, and have significantly contributed to numerous health fairs and wellness events within her local community. Additionally, Dr. Beverly has established and coordinated continuous quality improvement programs for several hospital sites, developed and implemented worksite wellness programs, and pioneered a mentoring program for women within 3 hospital organizations. She has published in professional journals, such as *The American Journal of Kidney Disease,* as well as popular print media inclusive of *Upscale* magazine, *Essence* magazine, and *Atlanta Journal Constitution.* As a committed member of the prestigious Sigma Iota Epsilon (SIE), Dr. Beverly continues to leverage her knowledge and experience to provide expert insight and practical perspective to interns, students of management, leaders, and corporate professionals.

To reach Dr. Beverly Hernandez, please e-mail: drbeverlyhernandez @gmail.com

CHAPTER 9

Innovative Recommendations for Assisting Homeless Students

Dr. Denise Thomas

The challenges that homeless people, especially children, must deal with on a daily basis are often overlooked. Between 700,000 to 800,000 people experience homelessness in this country any given night, and 2.5 to 3.5 million over the course of a year (National Alliance to End Homelessness 2004). Former President George W. Bush addressed ending chronic homelessness in his fiscal year 2003 budget. In 2003, at the U.S. Conference of Mayors, more than one hundred cities and some states committed themselves to developing a plan by 2004 to end chronic homelessness in the next 10 years. To date, no US city has been successful in ending the chronic homelessness. While significant research continues, there are some innovative recommendations that could be implemented to further assist school districts with providing information to homeless students and their families.

No one knows the exact number of homeless students in a given school district. Homeless numbers are based upon services provided to homeless students by the school district and other service providers. Not all of the homeless students are receiving supportive services. A thesis study was completed in 2005 by Dr. Denise Rudolph (Thomas) entitled: *A Descriptive Study to Determine the Perceptions of Providers and Beneficiaries related to the Stewart B.*

McKinney Homeless Assistance Act (McKinney-Vento). The purpose of thesis study was to determine if the school district (second largest in the country) provided to the homeless students the 14 services identified in the McKinney-Vento Act. Based upon the information provided from the 2005 Rudolph study, the school district studied was providing services to homeless students. However, the parents of homeless students stated they were not award of some of the services provided by the school district. Table 1, offers a list of services that should be provided to homeless students as required by law under the McKinney-Vento Act. The 2005 Rudolph study showed:

> The providers reported that ten of the fourteen services are offered more than 50 percent of the time. The schools do not provided information in the locations where the homeless are living. This is supported by the questionnaires results in which providers reported that out of thirty-two providers, eleven schools do not provide any information to any location where homeless students live. However, it appears that the schools will provide the services at the parents' request. (Rudolph, 2005, p. 87)

According to the McKinney-Vento Act (signed into law by President Ronald Reagan in 1987), the children have a right to these services and the schools are required to make an effort to offer these services to children who are:

1. Excessively absent from school

2. Constantly receiving poor grades

3. Under dressed for the weather

4. Functioning below their grade level

5. Child appears to be chronically ill

6. Child displays any mental or psychological behavior that is inappropriate.

Any student presenting one or more of these characteristics should be a 'red flag' for any teacher and prompt the teacher to take some kind of action. The teacher could speak with the student and the parent(s) to determine if some services are needed to assist this student.

These are the services that should be provided to children who are homeless according to the McKinney-Vento Homeless Assistance Act. The problem arises when school districts do not have the funding to provide these services for homeless students. In addition, some of the parents of homeless students are not aware that these resources are available for their children.

Table 1 offers a list of services where the parents ranked the frequency in which they received the services from the schools. The scale of frequency is: 1= Never, 2=Rarely, 3=Occasionally, 4= Fairly Often, 5= Often, 6=Almost Always, 7=Always.

TABLE 1: FREQUENCY OF SERVICES REPORTED BY PARENTS

Services Provided by School Districts	Ranking
1. After school tutoring.	3
2. Students' needs are evaluated and students are referred to other programs for assistance.	3
3. Professional training and other activities are developed, provided and/or implemented to assist coordinators and teachers in understand the special needs of homeless students.	4
4. Students are referred to medical, dental, mental and/or other health services, whenever necessary.	3

5.	Transportation is provided for students to attend school.	3
6.	Early childhood programs are available to assist children, such as preschool, Head Start, Even Start, pre-kindergarten.	3
7.	Programs are available to assist students before and after school with mentoring, assistance with homework and summer school.	4
8.	The school district obtains and transfers records necessary to enroll students. For example, immunization and academic records.	4
9.	Parents are given educational training or provided information concerning their children's rights and available resources.	4
10.	Services are coordinated between schools and other agencies providing services, such as, medical services, Girls and Boys club, YMCA, etc.	3
11.	When necessary, students and parents are providing information and referral for services concerning violence prevention and domestic violence counseling, etc.	3
12.	Schools should provide school supplies such as backpacks, uniforms, notebooks and clothing for physical education.	3
13.	Schools should provide information at local shelters, missions and other agencies were homeless families seek services.	3
14.	School district should provide emergency assistance to help children attend school.	3

(**Reprinted with permission, Rudolph, 2005, p. 93)

It is interesting to note that the parents of homeless children gave a ranking of 4 (fairly often) or less out of a possible 7 (Always). These services are *not consistently* provided to help homeless students stay in school and to develop patterns of success. Without these services student are at a greater disadvantage or risk of not graduating from high school.

Innovative Recommendations

A disconnect happens when the parents of homeless students are not aware of the services being offered by the schools to assist their children. Since the services are offered approximately 50% of the time, and the services are received occasionally, the following innovative strategies may assistance schools in any school district with providing these valuable services 100% of the time. Some of these suggestions will also not significantly increase costs to the school districts to implement, which is a help to the fiscally tight budget of the present economy.

1. Create a packet of information for children

2. Create a packet of information for the parents

3. Create a clothing closet

4. Keep homeless children in the same school

5. Present information at a general assembly

6. Include the information in the daily announcements

7. Place some general information on the back of each pupil's student ID cards

8. Promote the information on public television

9. Teachers: Assist with homework and create support groups

10. Create a brochure

Since parents reported only occasionally receiving or even knowing about the services, implementing one or more of these suggestions would increase the likelihood that the parents would request these services for their children. These services will greatly increase the homeless students' chances of improving in school.

An information packet could be created with an information sheet that explains to children some of the services that are available to them. The information should be written for the appropriate age group. Since teachers may not be able to identify which students are homeless, this information could be reviewed or explained in class or perhaps sent 'home' with the child to give to their parents.

A school could create an information packet for parents. A one-page information sheet could be created and sent home with the child to give to their parents. This information should be brief and simply stated. The parents would have a greater chance of receiving the information and no additional cost will be incurred by the school district with the minimal exception of the expense of purchasing paper and printing cost.

School districts could establish clothing closets for students. If the high school students donate good clothing to middle schools student in other areas, homeless students would have the latest styles to wear and no one would know. In Los Angeles, California, some of the WorkSource Centers, funded by the Workforce Investment Act, have established clothing closet for their participants. These clothing closets have assisted participants in getting jobs by helping them dress appropriately for job interviews.

When families become homeless, they often move from one location to another. Perhaps they are living in a motel or on the street, until they can obtain some kind of low rent housing. This also may mean that the children are changing schools frequently. Keep students in the same school they were attending before they became homeless. Children need to have stability in their lives. School can be that place. The Local Educational Agency Requirement under the McKinney-Vento Act 2002 states: children and youth, "are promptly provided necessary services describe in subsection (g) (4), including transportation, to allow homeless childe and youth to exercise their choices of schools under subsection (g) (3) (A)" (para. 4).

Schools could present information at their general assembly. Schools often have pep-rallies (school assemblies) and this would be a good place to give some information to students. The school could place fliers in a location within the office so that if a child were interested they would be able to get the information to take home to their parents. Also, the school could select one of their coordinators to be the go-to person for more information. This person should be introduced at the assembly as well.

Most schools have daily announcements that are given to all students at the beginning of the school day. Information could be included at least one day each week. The announcement would give information to the entire student population to help all students to understand that they can get some assistance whenever they need it. The announcement should identify whom they should speak to for some additional information or assistance.

Schools could place some general information on a label and place it on the back of the pupil's student identification card. At Perkins Middle School in Clark County School District, each student wears an ID card. Parents who help their children dress could see the information and seek assistance if needed.

Many television stations have public access television. The schools could create public announcements. This would allow information for homeless students to be broadcasted over a large area. More individuals and families would be able to receive the information for themselves or give the information to a family in need.

Teachers could allow a few minutes at the end of each class to ensure that the student is able to complete his or her homework with little to no assistance. Also, teachers could group students into teams, so that the homeless student would have a support group or someone to help him or her after school.

A brochure, providing all necessary information could be created. The Clark County School District in Nevada has developed a well thought out brochure for their students. The brochure is called: *Clark County School District, Title I Hope, Homeless Outreach Program for Education.* This brochure is colorful and easy to read. The brochure provides a great deal of valuable information for homeless students and their parents. In addition, when you open the brochure, in the center you will find emergency numbers and the names of agencies to contact for assistance. A website is also provided. The brochure gives information on housing, emergency food, dental care, day care, shelters, legal services and more. Step one is providing critical support services that will significantly help homeless students. Step two is disseminating information so that the services are well utilized.

Conclusion

The problems associated with homelessness, are easier to address earlier in life. Innovative approaches are needed to minimize the impact on student and to provide the support that will make it much easier for them to be successful. It is important for the success of homeless students that their parents, caregivers or guardians, be provided with the information and support discussed here. All of these suggestions may not work for each school, and all of the innovative recommendations may not be possible for every school district; however, implementing innovative support services would increase awareness among homeless families and the ability for them to utilize such services. Also, implementing these services could increase the chances of students staying in school and increasing their test scores. Children are the future leaders. We must give them a strong foundation for their success and ours.

References

Associated Press. (2006). *The meanest cities to homeless ranked.* Retrieved from http://abclocal.go.com/wpvi/story?section=news/national_world&id=3787609

Homeless statistics. (2000). Retrieved from http://www.homeless.org.au/statistics/#US

Hunger and homelessness survey. (2009). Retrieved from: http://www.usmayors.org/pressreleases/uploads/USCMHungercompleteWEB2009.pdf

McKinney-Vento Homeless Education Assistance District Liaison Guidance. (2005). Retrieved from http://www.opi.mt.gov/pdf/homeless/LiaisonGuidance.pdf

National Coalition for the Homeless. (2008). *What is homelessnes?* Retrieved from http://www.nationalhomeless.org/factsheets/Fact%20Sheet%20for%20CollegeStudents.pdf

Oracle ThinkQuest Education Foundation. (2003). *Homeless children by Maggie.* Retrieved from http://library.thinkquest.org/03oct/00921/homeless.htm

Rudolph, D. (2005). *A descriptive study to determine the perceptions of providers and beneficiaries related to the Stewart B. McKinney Act.* (Doctoral dissertation). Available from ProQuest Dissertations and Theses database. (UMI No. 3184786)

U. S. Department of Housing and Urban Development. (2007). *McKinney-Vento Act.* Retrieved from http://www.hud.gov/offices/cpd/homeless/lawsandregs/mckv.cfm

U.S. Department of Housing and Urban Development. (2008). *Homeless prevention and rapid re-housing program.* Retrieved from http://portal.hud.gov/portal/page/portal/HUD/topics/homelessness

About the Author

Dr. Denise Thomas, formerly Dr. Denise Rudolph, holds several accredited degrees: an Associate Degree (AS) in Business Management from Franklin University, a Bachelor Degree (BS) in Business Administration from University of Phoenix, a Master Degree (MAM) in Management with an emphasis in Human Resources from the University of Redlands and a Doctorate of Education Degree in Organizational Leadership from the University of La Verne.

She also attended Union Bible College and is a licensed minister under The Family Church International, Dr. Donnie Williams, Presiding Bishop. Dr. Thomas and her husband, Elder Dresden Thomas are the Pastors of Jesus Saves Family Church of Las Vegas. Dr. Denise has two children, Vinson and Shanese Winfrey, and she is also a singer and songwriter of contemporary Gospel music.

Dr. Denise is currently a faculty member and Area Chair for the University of Phoenix, College of Arts and Science, Las Vegas Campus. She is the Director of Operations and Administrative Services for DFT Trading Company. She is currently working on the following books: *What to Do When You are Homeless, De-Programming for Abused Individuals,* and *Love After Age 50.*

To reach Dr. Denise Thomas for information on any of these topics please e-mail: dr.denisethomas@embarqmail.com

The Refractive Thinker®: The Concept—Where Do We Go from Here?

Dr. Cheryl A. Lentz

Our Mission Statement

The purpose of The Refractive Thinker® is to facilitate the publishing needs of doctoral scholars while collaboratively sharing the expense and the promotion.

Since the first volume of *The Refractive Thinker® Doctoral Anthology* series was published, I have been continually asked several questions, what is a refractive thinker®, how did the concept of refractive thinking begin, and what value does this add to the concept of *thinking* and *critical thinking*? The goal of this writing is to offer more of an in-depth analysis and discussion of what this concept is as we go in search of the elusive refractive thinker as part of the mission statement for this project.

Who is a Refractive Thinker®?

A refractive thinker is someone that is insatiable with their curiosity. They are not satisfied within current conventional parameters or the prevailing wisdom. They are frustrated by provincial thinking or analysis. They do not follow the crowd. Instead the crowd follows them. They do not like the constraints of only an either/or option where many believe there are only two options: *in the box* or *out of the box* boundaries. Instead of merely preferring to color outside of the lines, they prefer to redefine the very rules that constrain the lines themselves, questioning the structure itself. Refractive thinkers are those that feel constrained by boundaries. They prefer to not only test the limits but expand well beyond them.

Refractive thinkers are often the ones that create the new business models, those who make new scientific discoveries, and those who offer never before held theories to try explaining existing or new phenomenon. They are the explorers of thoughts, those willing to ask the right questions that often take them—and those following them—in new and unchartered waters. The refractive thinker is comfortable with limitless boundaries and the suspensions of rules. Refractive thinkers are the pioneers such as Sir Isaac Newton, Albert Einstein, Benjamin Franklin, Leonardo da Vinci, Mohandas Gandhi, and Madame Curie. They are those that not only ask *why*, but *why not* when attempting to unlock the secrets of the universe and beyond.

How Did Refractive Thinking Begin?

Having taught critical thinking in the collegiate academic classroom for nearly 10 years, I found myself as an instructor feeling that somehow our critical thinking discussion was incomplete and inadequate—as if something were missing. There was always this nagging question in the back of my mind that wanted to know if there was something more. What I am trying to get away from is the invariable discussion of the dichotomy of either/or, black or white, either 'your way' or 'my way' type of limited thinking. My students seem to embrace the zero sum gain of *I can only win if you lose* type of mentality. Society seems to be conditioned to think there are *only* two extremes where thinking is either *inside* the box and everything else or critical thinking is *outside* the box. Somehow as a society, we are uncomfortable without having labels or descriptors, if only for a short time and boy do we love that proverbial box.

Story Time

To answer that nagging voice in the back of my mind, to discover what was missing, I offer the following short story for explanation.

Years ago, I attended a seminar of about 15 people with two facilitators where we had 10 days to brainstorm and address specific issues the company we all worked for at the time were experiencing. The first 3 days were agonizing for me. In the corporate setting, I would try very hard to keep the professor part of my personality from sharing too much of the spotlight. However by the third day of this group trying to put 10 lbs into a 5 lb box, I had simply hit my limit and the professor in me began to slowly emerge.

I asked for a few minutes of 'air time' from the facilitators and made my plea to the group to stop going down this road. I offered them a different perspective instead. I gave them permission to think *beyond* the box, beyond limits, beyond boundaries. What happened next was nothing short of amazing. Wow—if you could have been in the room at the time, as the shift that took place was amazing, how the energy simply shifted at that one specific moment in time. This is where the refractive thinker found its humble beginnings— completely unbeknownst to me at the time.

Once I took the rules and *perceived* boundaries away, and gave my fellow attendees permission to allow the situation to dictate its form, instead of the reverse, where form was dictating its solution; the energy in the room changed instantaneously. I simply gave us all permission to let go and to let our creativity and thinking lead us to follow its own path.

How Does Refractive Thinking Relate to Critical and Creative Thinking?

If thinking is *inside* the box, and critical thinking is *outside* the box, then refractive thinking is *beyond* the box. This invariably begs the question where and how creative thinking fits into the picture. Creative thinking and refractive thinking are indeed close cousins. Think of creative thinking as the initial *process*—the brainstorming, the mind mapping, the unique ways of incorporating different ways to look at something—the ability to think of ingenious, remarkable, and usual solutions.

Typically this is the point at which thinking then stops. While many of my students use these tools and techniques—their use is still *within their perceived boundaries* of either in or out of the box, coloring in or outside of the lines—the either or dichotomy. The limits seemingly still exist despite these additional techniques and perspective.

Instead, refractive thinking is design to look toward existing *without* boundaries, suspending judgment, freeing one's mind to be limitless. Creative thinking is often a challenge because we are still thinking along the lines of what are the rules and can I offer solutions either within the rules (which is what this seminar offered) or to break the rules entirely. Refractive thinking goes beyond the rules, the very instance between rules and no rules, simply existing where one suspends and resists any type of confinement, boundaries, labels, or parameters of any kind. This free thinking without any convention at all is something that few truly can obtain.

Einstein was one of the rare few who could truly think thoughts that had not been previously considered. He began to think of thinking as trying to decipher behavior that simply did not follow conventional thinking or the prevailing wisdom. Initially, few could grasp the radically different concepts he put forth. Much like during the time of Sir Isaac Newton or perhaps even further when the earth was believed to once be flat, these are the pioneers of thought—the true pioneers of refractive thinking.

Refractive thinking requires a leap of faith, belief in the process whereby suspending judgment, labels, boundaries, and any type of traditionally held constraints, that one's mind can begin to simply ponder the improbable, reflect on the impossible, bend thought beyond the plausible, to truly explore the infinite—to infinite and beyond.

Descartes offers the often quoted phrase: *"I think therefore I am."* Allow me to continue his thought by adding, "I critically think *to be,* I refractively think *to change the world"* (Lentz, 2009). My goal in academia and within the business world is to help students and adult learners develop their critical thinking skills to see what is already there with a slightly different lens from a new perspective; to learn to question everything they see-to return to the oft favorite phrase of a child—the curiosity driven question, *why.* What a shame that as adults we lose this idyllic curiosity and wonder.

The goal of refractive thinking is to embrace the post modernism guise of being able to hold divergent points of view and theory *simultaneously,* building a foundation of duality. Society is uncomfortable with simultaneous duality—the thought that two divergent boundaries can exist and both can be correct—*from their point of view* is challenging to wrap one's arms around. Dealing within this not only duality but multiplicity of meaning simultaneously is where refractive thinking exists, expands, and offers a new contemplation of thought. The goal is to be able to simply exist within a modality of asking *why* and *why not,* to challenge conventional wisdom to suggest *what if?* The goal is to build the capacity to understanding limitlessness and beyond what we think of currently as infinite wisdom.

What is it that prevents most people from achieving this state?

Why is it easier to cling to the safety of the confines of the proverbial box allowing only the dichotomy of opposites, or either or extremes? Instead, why not break this cycle of fear and simply stop? Choose to simply exist and go well beyond the box. Perhaps the solution is not a box *at all.* Instead, this is yet some free form that is fluid and dynamic, without an exact or known label. Can we exist without having to define the parameters of that existence definitely? This is the quest of the refractive thinker—to discover the yet unknown and to realize that one cannot put new ideas into old constructs.

About the Editor

Southern Nevadan internationally published author Dr. Cheryl A. Lentz holds several accredited degrees; a Bachelor of Arts (BA) from the University of Illinois, Urbana-Champaign; a Master of Science in International Relations (MSIR) from Troy University; and a Doctorate of Management (DM) in Organizational Leadership from University of Phoenix School of Advanced Studies.

Dr. Cheryl, affectionately known as 'Doc C' to her students, is a university professor on faculty with Embry-Riddle University, Colorado State University-Global, The University of the Rockies, and University of Phoenix where she also serves on several doctoral committees and is a faculty mentor. Dr. Cheryl also offers expertise in editing for APA style for graduate thesis and doctoral dissertations.

Dr. Cheryl is also an active member of Alpha Sigma Alpha Sorority.

Additional published works include her dissertation: *Strategic Decision Making in Organizational Performance: A Quantitative Study of Employee Inclusiveness, The Golden Palace Theory of Management, Journey Outside the Golden Palace, The Refractive Thinker: Vol. I: An Anthology of Doctoral Learners, Vol. II: Research Methodology, Vol. III. Change Management, and Volume III: Ethics, Leadership, and Globalization.* For additional details, please visit her website: www.drcheryllentz.com

To reach Dr. Cheryl Lentz for information on any of these topics, and please e-mail: drcheryllentz@gmail.com

Index

Other Books by the
The Refractive Thinker® Press

The Refractive Thinker®: Volume I: An Anthology of Higher Learning

The Refractive Thinker®: Volume II: Research Methodology

The Refractive Thinker®: Volume III: Change Management

The Refractive Thinker®: Volume IV: Ethics, Leadership, and Globalization

The Refractive Thinker®: Volume V: Strategy in Innovation

Available in e-book, Kindle®, Ipad®, Nook®, and Sony e-Reader, as well as individual e-chapters by author.

Coming Spring 2011

The Refractive Thinker®: Volume II: Research Methodology,
*   Second Edition*

MasterMinds: Graduate Anthology: Abstracts & Essays

Telephone orders: Call us at 877 298-5172

Fax Orders: Fax us at 877 298-5172

Email Orders: info@refractivethinker.com

Website orders: Please place orders through our website:
                www.refractivethinker.com

Postal Orders: The Refractive Thinker® Press
                9065 Big Plantation Avenue
                Las Vegas, NV 89143-5440   USA

Refractive
Thinker®
Press

from The Refractive Thinker® Press

The Refractive Thinker®: Volume III: Change Management

This next offering shares yet another glimpse into the scholarly works of these authors, specifically on the topic of change management. In addition to exploring various aspects of change management, the purpose of *The Refractive Thinker®* is also to serve the tenets of leadership. Leadership is not simply a concept outside of the self, but comes from within, defining our very essence; where the search to define leadership becomes our personal journey not yet a finite destination.

The Refractive Thinker®: Volume IV: Ethics, Leadership, and Globalization

The purpose of this next volume in *The Refractive Thinker®* series is to share yet another glimpse into the scholarly works of these authors, specifically on the topics of ethics, leadership, and concerns within the global landscape of business. I invite you to join with me as we venture forward to showcase the authors of Volume IV, and continue to celebrate the accomplishments of these doctoral scholars affiliated with many phenomenal institutions of higher learning.

For more information, please visit our website: www.refractivethinker.com

Please send the following books:

❏ *The Refractive Thinker®: Volume I:*
   An Anthology of Higher Learning

❏ *The Refractive Thinker®: Volume II:*
   Research Methodology

❏ *The Refractive Thinker®: Volume III:*
   Change Management

❏ *The Refractive Thinker®: Volume IV:*
   Ethics, Leadership, and Globalization

❏ *The Refractive Thinker®: Volume V:*
   Strategy in Innovation

Please contact the Refractive Thinker® Press for book prices, e-book prices, and shipping.

Individual e-chapters available by author: $3.95 (plus applicable tax).
   www.refractivethinker.com

Please send more FREE information:

❏ Speaking Engagements

❏ The Refractive Thinker® Press Educational Seminars

❏ Consulting

Join our Mailing List

Name: _____

Address: _____

City: _____ State: _____ Zip: _____

Telephone: _____ Email: ._____

Sales tax: NV Residents please add 8.1% sales tax

Shipping: *Please see our website for shipping rates.*

Refractive
Thinker®
Press

Please send the following books:

❏ *The Refractive Thinker®: Volume I:*
  An Anthology of Higher Learning

❏ *The Refractive Thinker®: Volume II:*
  Research Methodology

❏ *The Refractive Thinker®: Volume III:*
  Change Management

❏ *The Refractive Thinker®: Volume IV:*
  Ethics, Leadership, and Globalization

❏ *The Refractive Thinker®: Volume V:*
  Strategy in Innovation

Please contact the Refractive Thinker® Press for book prices, e-book prices, and shipping.

Individual e-chapters available by author: $3.95 (plus applicable tax). www.refractivethinker.com

Please send more FREE information:

❏ Speaking Engagements

❏ The Refractive Thinker® Press Educational Seminars

❏ Consulting

Join our Mailing List

Name: _____

Address: _____

City: _____ State: _____ Zip: _____

Telephone: _____ Email: _____

Sales tax: NV Residents please add 8.1% sales tax

Shipping: *Please see our website for shipping rates.*

Refractive
Thinker®
Press

Participation in Future Volumes of
The Refractive Thinker® or MasterMinds

Yes I would like to participate in:

❑ **Doctoral Volume**(s) for a specific university or your organization:

Name: _____

Contact Person: _____

Telephone: _____ E-mail: _____

❑ **Graduate Volume**(s) MasterMinds for a specific university or your organization:

Name: _____

Contact Person: _____

Telephone: _____ E-mail: _____

❑ **Specialized Volume**(s) Business or Themed:

Name: _____

Contact Person: _____

Telephone: _____ E-mail: _____

Please mail or fax form to:

The Refractive Thinker® Press
9065 Big Plantation Ave.
Las Vegas, NV 89143-5440   USA
Fax: 877-298-5172
www.refractivethinker.com